Mocha on the Mount

Advancing the Ministries of the Gospel

AMG *Publishers*

God's Word to you is our highest calling.

SANDRA GLAHN

Coffee Cup Bible Studies
Mocha on the Mount

© 2006 by Sandra L. Glahn

Published by AMG Publishers. All Rights Reserved.

Published in association with the literary
agency of Alive Communications, Inc., 7860 Goddard Street, Suite 200,
Colorado Springs, Colorado, 80920

First Printing, 2006

ISBN: 0-89957-223-5

Editing and Proofreading: Rick Steele and Jonathan Wright
Interior Design: PerfecType, Nashville, Tennessee
Cover Design: Brian Woodief at ImageWright Marketing and Design,
Chattanooga, Tennessee

Printed in the United States of America
11 10 09 08 07 06 –D– 6 5 4 3 2 1

ACKNOWLEDGMENTS

When I think of those who have had some part in bringing this book to fruition, I can understand something of what Paul must have felt when he wrote, "For what thanks can we render to God for you in return for all the joy with which we rejoice before our God on your account?" (1 Thess. 3:9). Thanks are due to numerous people whom I cannot name due to space limitations, but I would be remiss if I failed to thank at least the following:

- Gary, my beloved husband and ministry partner, for his love and encouragement, for sharing with me his research notes on Jesus' teachings, and for designing and maintaining the web site component of the Coffee Cup series

- Professor Schuppe, who made the Sermon on the Mount come alive for the first time when I was a wide-eyed college freshman

- my other professors at the Washington Bible College and those at Dallas Theological Seminary who taught me to carefully but confidently handle the Word

- Dr. Elizabeth Inrig, who believed I could teach despite my youth long before I had the confidence to do so—and who, along with my husband, opened the doors for me to get a seminary education

- the women's Bible Study at Reinhardt Bible Church for their feedback when I initially taught this material. I am especially indebted to Glad Phillips and Nancy Moon—older women willing to teach the younger. Though they are now absent from the body and present with the Lord, their investment continues

- the gifted staff of Biblical Studies Press (bible.org), translators of the NET Bible, printed as the primary Scripture text in this book. Without the help of this essential ministry, the entire concept of the Coffee Cup Bible Studies would not be possible

- My agent-turned-publisher, Chip MacGregor, for guidance with the series concept and finding a home for it

- Virginia Swint and Karen Swint for careful editing and tireless encouragement

- Dan Penwell and Rick Steele of AMG for their enthusiasm for this project, their commitment to excellence, and their generous encouragement along the way

- those who are praying that God will use His word to change lives. Some day your works done in secret will be rewarded openly

- the Lord Jesus Christ, who bids us enter the kingdom clothed in His righteousness alone. Only by His grace do I stand. *Soli Deo Gloria.*

Introduction to the Coffee Cup Bible Studies

"The precepts of the LORD are right, rejoicing the heart;
The commandment of the LORD is pure, enlightening the eyes." (Psa. 19:8, NASB)

Congratulations! You have chosen wisely. By choosing to study the Bible, you are electing to spend time learning that which will rejoice the heart and enlighten the eyes.

And while any study in the Bible is time well spent, the Coffee Cup Bible Studies have some unique elements that set them apart from others. So before we get started, let's talk about some of those elements that will, we hope, help you maximize your study time.

Life Rhythms. Most participants in any Bible study have little problem keeping up during the weekdays, when they have a routine. Yet on the weekends there's a general "falling off." Thus, the Coffee Cup Bible Studies contain Monday-through-Friday Bible study questions, but the Saturday and Sunday segments consist of shorter, more passive readings that draw application and insight from the texts you'll be considering. Know that the days listed here are mere suggestions. Some find it preferable to attend a Bible study one day and follow a four-day-per-week study schedule along with weekend readings. Feel free to change the structure of days and assignments to best fit your own needs.

Community. The studies in the Coffee Cup series are ideal for group interaction. If you don't have a local group with which to meet, find a few friends and start one. Or connect with others through the **Mocha on the Mount** section of the author's web site (www.aspire2.com) and an associated site, where you can find and participate—if you like—by engaging in artistic expressions as you interact with the text. These vehicles give you opportunities to share with a wider community what you're learning. While each study is designed for group use, private questions not intended for group discussion appear in italic type.

Aesthetics. At the author's web site in a section designed for the Coffee Cup Bible Studies, you will find links to art that depicts what's being discussed—whether to Domenico Fetti's brilliant illustration of "The Parable of the Mote and the Beam" (1619), or woodcuts depicting Sermon-on-the-Mount teachings from the Protestant Reformation era, you'll find something to illustrate the concepts you're learning. And as mentioned, readers wanting to engage all five senses in their interaction with God's truth will find a link to a site set up for encouraging that very purpose.

Convenience. Rather than turning in the Bible to find the references, you'll find the entire text for each day included in each of the Coffee Cup Bible Studies (thanks to the Biblical Studies Foundation). While it's important to know our way around the Bible, the Coffee Cup series is designed this way so you can take it with you and study the Bible on the subway, at a coffee shop, in a doctors' waiting room, or on your lunch break. The chosen translation is the NET Bible, which is accessible via internet from virtually anywhere in the world. You can find more about it, along with numerous textual notes, at www.bible.org, which serves 3.5 million people worldwide.

The NET Bible is a modern translation from the ancient Greek, Hebrew, and Aramaic texts. Alumni and friends of Dallas Theological Seminary make up the core group of individuals behind the site, particularly the NET Bible translation project. Both the online and text versions of this Bible include 60,932 translators' notes and citations originating from more than 700 scholarly works.

Sensitivity to time-and-culture considerations. Many Bible studies skip what we call the "theological" step. That is, they go straight from observing and interpreting the words given to those in a different time and culture to applying in a modern-day setting. The result is sometimes misapplication (such as, "Paul told slaves to obey their masters so we need to obey our employers"). In the Coffee Cup Bible Studies, our aim is to be particularly sensitive to the audience to whom the "mail" was addressed and work to take the crucial step of separating what was intended for a limited audience from that which is for all audiences for all time (love God; love your neighbor).

Sensitivity to genres. Rather than crafting a series in which each study is structured exactly like all the others, each Coffee Cup Bible study is structured to offer the best consideration of the genre being examined—whether poetry, gospel, history, or narrative. The way we study Esther, a story, differs from how we might study Paul's epistle to the Ephesians or the poetry in Song of Songs. So while the studies may have similar elements, no two will be quite the same.

INTRODUCTION TO
MOCHA ON THE MOUNT

The Gospels of Matthew, Mark, Luke, and John record events in
the life of Jesus though which readers find selective rather than com-
plete biographies. Each Gospel writer seeks to show a different side of
Jesus. The Gospel of Matthew reveals Jesus as King and provides prin-
ciples for kingdom living. Matthew repeatedly uses the phrase "the
kingdom of heaven," particularly in the three chapters we'll explore in
depth. Other Gospel writers use "the kingdom of God," but Matthew,
like many good Jews, seems to shy away from coming out and using
the exalted and holy name of God. So the meanings of "kingdom of
heaven" and "kingdom of God," which is used in other Gospels,
appear to be the same.

In chapters five through seven of Matthew's Gospel we find the
Sermon on the Mount. Jesus delivers this sermon at the beginning
of His ministry, when He is popular and has a large following. His
message comes on the heels of John the Baptist's exhortation to
"bring fruits of repentance." Jesus is continuing the message "The
kingdom is at hand," and news of its entrance requirement—absolute
righteousness.

Those who listened, the "disciples," consisted of more than "the
twelve." The listeners followed Jesus and may or may not have
believed.

Those who followed Jesus and heard Him preach knew only the
teaching of religious leaders of their day, who interpreted the Law for

everyone. The leaders had led the people astray, and Jesus set out to make some needed corrections.

If Jesus was talking to Jewish followers looking for an earthly kingdom, how does His message apply to us, His followers in the Church? Entire theses have been written to address this question. But in short, Jesus was speaking to those who would be rightly related to God and heirs of the coming kingdom. They also needed to exhibit true righteousness and fruits of repentance. In these ways, we have so much in common with them that we can take to heart all of Jesus' teachings.

Jesus brought a message that differed significantly from what the people had heard. We begin by clarifying what His sermon is *not*:

- The Sermon on the Mount is not comprised of a list of dos and don'ts that, if followed, will ensure or aid one's entrance into the kingdom.
- The Sermon is not a message about how people must earn favor with God by good works alone.

Then what is it?

- It is a sermon in which Jesus gives the characteristics of the person who will enter His kingdom.
- It is a sermon in which Jesus shows how a person who is in right relationship to God should conduct his or her life and outlines the true fruits of repentance.

So follow Jesus as He enters the hill country west of Galilee and sits down. Whereas today's lecturers and preachers stand to speak, in Jesus' day the posture of a speaker in a synagogue or school was to sit. So we join Him on the side of a mountain with those who wonder, "Am I eligible to enter the kingdom of heaven?"

CONTENTS

Week 1
Lifestyles of the Rich: Matthew 5:1–16   1

Week 2
The Law Revisited: Matthew 5:17–48   27

Week 3
The Secret-Filled Life: Matthew 6:1–18   49

Week 4
About Storage: Matthew 6:19–34   64

Week 5
Sticking to a Single Standard: Matthew 7:1–12   81

Week 6
A Study in Contrasts: Matthew 7:13–29   104

WEEK 1 OF 6

Lifestyles of the Rich: Matthew 5:1–16

SUNDAY: LOOKING FOR BLISS IN THE WRONG PLACES

I read a sign not long ago that said, "The geek shall inherit the earth." In other words, the same nerd you used to mock in high school could turn out to be the next Bill Gates.

While the maker of the sign twisted Jesus' words—not a good thing—in some ways this sign and the teaching of Jesus from the Beatitudes have something in common: the truth that what we value now will get totally reversed in the future. The popular high school jock may grow up to be an unemployed slob while the geek grows up to be a CEO of a Fortune 500 company. And the person who has nothing in this life but who is rich toward God will end up owning the whole place in the future.

Think of what we usually consider blessing: We're blessed if we're rich; we're blessed to have food on the table; we're blessed that we rarely face the threat of dying for our faith.

Jesus takes such thinking and flips it. He says we're blessed if we're poor; we're blessed if we hunger; we're blessed if we're persecuted.

What? Why? Because apart from spiritual poverty, hunger, and the threat of death, we fail to see our deep need and call out to the only one who can ultimately help us.

Consider the proud Pharisee who thanked God he was unlike the sinning tax collector. Yet that tax collector, deeply aware of his own insufficient righteousness, cried out "Lord, have mercy!" In comparing himself with God and coming up far short, the tax collector found himself humbled and in need of God's mercy. And he became the object of God's favor (Luke 18:13–14).

Jesus develops the concept of reversal in His Sermon on the Mount. That reversal is seen in where he begins—with the Beatitudes.

Last week my ten-year-old daughter informed me that every sentence, in order to be a sentence, must have both a subject and a verb. Yet a few thousand years ago, Greek teachers helping students learn to write would have laid out no such requirement. That explains why we find only verbless phrases in the Beatitudes. They're full of exclamations, not sentences: "Blessed the poor in spirit! Blessed those who mourn! Blessed the persecuted!"

Such exclamations also occur frequently in the Old Testament, particularly in the Psalms. Think of how Psalm 1 begins: "Bléssed the person who does not walk in the counsel of the wicked." Again, we find no "be" verb in the original. Whereas sometimes ideas get "lost in translation," in this case, "be" verbs got added.

What does it mean to be blessed (a better translation than "happy")? Happiness depends on external circumstances—I got a new job, I got engaged, my relationships are going well. But blessing depends on being rightly related to God despite external circumstances. Horatio Spafford, though his daughters had just drowned in a boating accident, was still able to write, "It is well with my soul." I seriously doubt he felt happy. Yet he knew he was blessed. Lady Juliana of Norwich, writing in the fourteenth century, said, "All shall be well and all shall be well and all manner of thing shall be well."

Jesus' message would never fly on Madison Avenue: Sign up for the Christian life. Come, be poor and mourn and die!

"Honestly, I want to be like Christ," writes Ken Gire in *The Reflective Life*.

> But honestly I want to be like the Christ who turned
> water into wine, not the Christ who thirsted on a
> cross. I want to be the clothed Christ, not the one

whose garment was stripped and gambled away. I want to be the Christ who fed the five thousand, not the one who hungered for forty days in the wilderness. . . . This is the dark side of Christianity, the side we don't see when we sign up. That if we want to be like Christ, we have to embrace both sides of His life. What else could it mean when the Bible talks about "the fellowship of His suffering"? How could we enter that fellowship apart from suffering? How could we truly know the Man of Sorrows acquainted with grief if we had not ourselves known grief and sorrow?[1]

When we're spiritually hungry, persecuted, and mourning over our sin, we're more likely to see our need. In contrast, when we sense we have no needs, we're self-sufficient. Isaiah saw the Lord and cried out, "Woe is me! I am a man of unclean lips" (Isaiah 6:1). The moment he saw God, he recognized his own sinfulness. For him it was the worst of times, it was the best of times.

Are you rich or needy?

"Blessed are the poor in spirit, for the kingdom of heaven belongs to them" (Matt. 5:3).

MONDAY: OVERVIEW

1. Pray for the Lord to reveal himself through His Word to you. Then read "The Sermon on the Mount" in Matthew 5–7.

Matthew 5

5:1 When he saw the crowds, he went up the mountain. After he sat down his disciples came to him. **5:2** Then he began to teach them by saying:

5:3 "Blessed are the poor in spirit, for the kingdom of heaven belongs to them.

5:4 "Blessed are those who mourn, for they will be comforted.

---

[1] Ken Gire, *The Reflective Life* (Colorado Springs, CO: Chariot Victor Publishing, 1998), as quoted in *Kindred Spirit* (Dallas, TX: Dallas Theological Seminary, Spring 2005), 29:1, back cover.

5:5 "Blessed are the meek, for they will inherit the earth.

5:6 "Blessed are those who hunger and thirst for righteousness, for they will be satisfied.

5:7 "Blessed are the merciful, for they will be shown mercy.

5:8 "Blessed are the pure in heart, for they will see God.

5:9 "Blessed are the peacemakers, for they will be called the children of God.

5:10 "Blessed are those who are persecuted for righteousness, for the kingdom of heaven belongs to them.

5:11 "Blessed are you when people insult you and persecute you and say all kinds of evil things about you falsely on account of me. **5:12** Rejoice and be glad because your reward is great in heaven, for they persecuted the prophets before you in the same way.

5:13 "You are the salt of the earth. But if salt loses its flavor, how can it be made salty again? It is no longer good for anything except to be thrown out and trampled on by people. **5:14** You are the light of the world. A city located on a hill cannot be hidden. **5:15** People do not light a lamp and put it under a basket but on a lampstand, and it gives light to all in the house. **5:16** In the same way, let your light shine before people, so that they can see your good deeds and give honor to your Father in heaven.

5:17 "Do not think that I have come to abolish the law or the prophets. I have not come to abolish these things but to fulfill them. **5:18** I tell you the truth, until heaven and earth pass away not the smallest letter or stroke of a letter will pass from the law until everything takes place. **5:19** So anyone who breaks one of the least of these commands and teaches others to do so will be called least in the kingdom of heaven, but whoever obeys them and teaches others to do so will be called great in the kingdom of heaven. **5:20** For I tell you, unless your righteousness goes beyond that of the experts in the law and the Pharisees, you will never enter the kingdom of heaven.

5:21 "You have heard that it was said to an older generation, '*Do not murder*,' and 'whoever murders will be subjected to judgment.' **5:22** But I say to you that anyone who is angry with a brother will be subjected to judgment. And whoever insults a brother will be brought before the council, and whoever says 'Fool' will be sent to fiery hell. **5:23** So then, if you bring your gift to the altar and there remember that your brother has something against you, **5:24** leave your gift there in front of the altar. First go and be reconciled to your brother and then come and present your gift. **5:25** Reach agreement quickly with your accuser while on the way to court, or he may hand you over to the judge, and the judge hand you over to the warden, and you will be thrown into prison. **5:26** I tell you the truth, you will never get out of there until you have paid the last penny!

5:27 "You have heard that it was said, '*Do not commit adultery*.' **5:28** But I say to you that whoever looks at a woman to desire her has already committed adultery with her in his heart. **5:29** If your right eye causes you to sin, tear it out and throw it away! It is better to lose one of your members than to have your whole body thrown into hell. **5:30** If your right hand causes you to sin, cut it off and throw it away! It is better to lose one of your members than to have your whole body go into hell.

5:31 "It was said, '*Whoever divorces his wife must give her a legal document*.' **5:32** But I say to you that everyone who divorces his wife, except for immorality, makes her commit adultery, and whoever marries a divorced woman commits adultery.

5:33 "Again, you have heard that it was said to an older generation, '*Do not break an oath, but fulfill your vows to the Lord*.' **5:34** But I say to you, do not take oaths at all—not by heaven, because it is the throne of God, **5:35** not by earth, because it is his footstool, and not by Jerusalem, because it is the city of the great King. **5:36** Do not take an oath by your head, because you are not able to make one hair white or black. **5:37** Let your word be 'Yes, yes' or 'No, no.' More than this is from the evil one.

5:38 "You have heard that it was said, '*An eye for an eye and a tooth for a tooth*.' **5:39** But I say to you, do not resist the evildoer. But whoever strikes you on the right cheek, turn the other to him as well. **5:40** And if someone wants to sue you and to take your tunic, give him your coat also. **5:41** And if anyone forces you to go one mile, go with him two. **5:42** Give to the one who asks you, and do not reject the one who wants to borrow from you.

5:43 "You have heard that it was said, '*Love your neighbor*' and 'hate your enemy.' **5:44** But I say to you, love your enemy and pray for those who persecute you, **5:45** so that you may be like your Father in heaven, since he causes the sun to rise on the evil and the good, and sends rain on the righteous and the unrighteous. **5:46** For if you love those who love you, what reward do you have? Even the tax collectors do the same, don't they? **5:47** And if you only greet your brothers, what more do you do? Even the Gentiles do the same, don't they? **5:48** So then, be perfect, as your heavenly Father is perfect.

Matthew 6

6:1 "Be careful not to display your righteousness merely to be seen by people. Otherwise you have no reward with your Father in heaven. **6:2** Thus whenever you do charitable giving, do not blow a trumpet before you, as the hypocrites do in synagogues and on streets so that people will praise them. I tell you the truth, they have their reward. **6:3** But when you do your giving, do not let your left hand know what your right hand is doing, **6:4** so that your gift may be in secret. And your Father, who sees in secret, will reward you.

6:5 "Whenever you pray, do not be like the hypocrites, because they love to pray while standing in synagogues and on street corners so that people can see them. Truly I say to you, they have their reward. **6:6** But whenever you pray, go into your room, close the door, and pray to your Father in secret. And your Father, who sees in secret, will reward you. **6:7** When you pray, do not babble repetitiously like the Gentiles, because they think that by their many words they will be heard. **6:8** Do not be like them, for your Father knows what you need before you ask him. **6:9** So pray this way: Our Father in heaven, may your name be honored,

6:10 may your kingdom come, may your will be done on earth as it is in heaven.

6:11 Give us today our daily bread,

6:12 and forgive us our debts, as we ourselves have forgiven our debtors.

6:13 And do not lead us into temptation, but deliver us from the evil one.

6:14 "For if you forgive others their sins, your heavenly Father will also forgive you. **6:15** But if you do not forgive others, your Father will not forgive you your sins.

6:16 "When you fast, do not look sullen like the hypocrites, for they make their faces unattractive so that people will see them fasting. I tell you the truth, they have their reward. **6:17** When you fast, put oil on your head and wash your face, **6:18** so that it will not be obvious to others when you are fasting, but only to your Father who is in secret. And your Father, who sees in secret, will reward you.

6:19 "Do not accumulate for yourselves treasures on earth, where moth and rust destroy and where thieves break in and steal.

6:20 But accumulate for yourselves treasures in heaven, where moth and rust do not destroy, and thieves do not break in and steal. **6:21** For where your treasure is, there your heart will be also.

6:22 "The eye is the lamp of the body. If then your eye is healthy, your whole body will be full of light. **6:23** But if your eye is diseased, your whole body will be full of darkness. If then the light in you is darkness, how great is the darkness!

6:24 "No one can serve two masters, for either he will hate the one and love the other, or he will be devoted to the one and despise the other. You cannot serve God and money.

6:25 "Therefore I tell you, do not worry about your life, what you will eat or drink, or about your body, what you will wear. Isn't there more to life than food and more to the body than clothing? **6:26** Look at the birds in the sky: They do not sow, or reap, or gather into barns, yet your heavenly Father feeds them. Aren't you more valuable than they are? **6:27** And which of you by worrying can add even one hour to his life? **6:28** Why do you worry about clothing? Think about how the flowers of the field grow; they do not work or spin. **6:29** Yet I tell you that not even Solomon in all his glory was clothed like one of these! **6:30** And if this is how God clothes the wild grass, which is here today and tomorrow is tossed into the fire to heat the oven, won't he clothe you even more, you people of little faith? **6:31** So then, don't worry saying, 'What will we eat?' or 'What will we drink?' or 'What will we wear?' **6:32** For the unconverted pursue these things, and your heavenly Father knows that you need them. **6:33** But above all pursue his kingdom and righteousness, and all these things will be given to you as well. **6:34** So then, do not worry about tomorrow, for tomorrow will worry about itself. Today has enough trouble of its own.

Matthew 7

7:1 "Do not judge so that you will not be judged. **7:2** For by the standard you judge you will be judged, and the measure you use will be the measure you receive. **7:3** Why do you see the speck in your brother's eye, but fail to see the beam of wood in your own? **7:4** Or how can you say to your brother, 'Let me remove the speck from your eye,' while there is a beam in your own? **7:5** You hypocrite! First remove the beam from your own eye, and then you can see clearly to remove the speck from your brother's eye. **7:6** Do not give what is holy to dogs or throw your pearls before pigs; otherwise they will trample them under their feet and turn around and tear you to pieces.

7:7 "Ask and it will be given to you; seek and you will find; knock and the door will be opened for you. **7:8** For everyone who asks receives, and the one who seeks finds, and to the one who knocks, the door will be opened. **7:9** Is there anyone among you who, if his son asks for bread, will give him a stone? **7:10** Or if he asks for a fish, will give him a snake? **7:11** If you then, although you are evil, know how to give good gifts to your children, how much more will your Father in heaven give good gifts to those who ask him! **7:12** In everything, treat others as you would want them to treat you, for this fulfills the law and the prophets.

7:13 "Enter through the narrow gate, because the gate is wide and the way is spacious that leads to destruction, and there are many who enter through it. **7:14** But the gate is narrow and the way is difficult that leads to life, and there are few who find it.

7:15 "Watch out for false prophets, who come to you in sheep's clothing but inwardly are voracious wolves. **7:16** You will recognize them by their fruit. Grapes are not gathered from thorns or figs from thistles, are they? **7:17** In the same way, every good tree bears good fruit, but the bad tree bears bad fruit. **7:18** A good tree is not able to bear bad fruit, nor a bad tree to bear good fruit. **7:19** Every tree that does not bear good fruit is cut down and thrown into the fire. **7:20** So then, you will recognize them by their fruit.

7:21 "Not everyone who says to me, 'Lord, Lord,' will enter into the kingdom of heaven—only the one who does the will of my Father in heaven. **7:22** On that day, many will say to me, 'Lord, Lord, didn't we prophesy in your name, and in your name cast out demons and do many powerful deeds?' **7:23** Then I will declare to them, 'I never knew you. Go away from me, you lawbreakers!'

7:24 "Everyone who hears these words of mine and does them is like a wise man who built his house on rock. **7:25** The rain fell, the flood came, and the winds beat against that house, but it did not collapse because it had been founded on rock. **7:26** Everyone who hears these words of mine and does not do them is like a foolish man who built his house on sand. **7:27** The rain fell, the flood came, and the winds beat against that house, and it collapsed; it was utterly destroyed!"

7:28 When Jesus finished saying these things, the crowds were amazed by his teaching, **7:29** because he taught them like one who had authority, not like their experts in the law.

2. You've just read some of Jesus' key teachings. His message focuses on Kingdom values. Go back and mark with a highlighter all references to "kingdom."

3. The things we value . . .

A. What are some standards by which we tend to measure status?

_____

_____

_____

B. What does Jesus say will be valued in the Kingdom?

_____

_____

_____

C. According to Jesus' teachings, how should we measure true success?

_____

_____

_____

_____

4. How does Jesus say one enters the Kingdom (5:20; 7:13–14, 21)?

_____

_____

_____

5. According to Jesus' words, what is the appropriate view of material possessions (6:19–34)?

_____

_____

_____

_____

6. On what do you spend most of your time and energy? How do your priorities line up with those Jesus sets forth?

_____

_____

_____

_____

7. Spend some time praying that the Lord will transform you and your values.

TUESDAY: THE POOR, THE MOURNING, THE MEEK

Jesus had a message for the people who followed the religious leaders of His day (the scribes and Pharisees): "Repent!"

John the Baptist, who came before Him, preached repentance. And Jesus sent His disciples out with the same message.

The Sermon on the Mount shows what's involved in repentance. The central idea seems to be "You're not ready for the kingdom of heaven—your righteousness is insufficient." Up to this point, the people would have looked to their spiritual leaders and thought, "Blessed are the big shots, the happy, those of whom others have spoken well." Jesus lets the crowds know they've gotten it backwards. Their standard must be even higher than that of popular spiritual big shots.

He begins with the Beatitudes. The format He follows is "Blessed are X, for they shall X." Every word in this structure has significance. To be blessed is to be envied. "For" tells why they're blessed. "They shall" is passive, suggesting that God does the action.

1. Re-read Matthew 5:3–5.

> **5:3** "Blessed are the poor in spirit, for the kingdom of heaven belongs to them.
>
> **5:4** "Blessed are those who mourn, for they will be comforted.
>
> **5:5** "Blessed are the meek, for they will inherit the earth."

2. What is the first qualification of Kingdom dwellers, and what do they possess (5:3)?

_____

_____

_____

_____

3. When Jesus says "poor in spirit," He's not speaking of financial destitution. What kind of poverty does He mean? Why do you think the list starts with this quality?

_____

_____

_____

_____

4. Pray for God to help you see your status as a beggar who recognizes his or her poverty before Him—to empty you of your self-righteousness, pride over moral self-esteem, and spiritual arrogance. Ask Him to help you see your state of spiritual impoverishment in the face of His holiness.

5. What's the second qualification of Kingdom dwellers, and what are they promised? (5:4). (Often this verse is quoted to those who have lost a loved one, but in the context it's about a specific kind of grieving—mourning over one's own sin.)

_____

_____

_____

6. Picture the grief that comes with a loss. What do grieving people do? What evidence do they give of their pain?

_____

_____

_____

7. Read Ecclesiastes 7:2–4 and consider what it says about mourning.

> **Ecclesiastes 7:2** It is better to go to a funeral than a feast. For death is the destiny of every person, and the living should take this to heart.
>
> **7:3** Sorrow is better than laughter, because sober reflection is good for the heart.
>
> **7:4** The heart of the wise is in the house of mourning, but the heart of fools is in the house of merrymaking.

According to the text, why is it better to go to a house of mourning than of feasting?

_____

_____

_____

_____

8. As mentioned, sometimes sympathy cards quote Jesus' promise that all who mourn will be comforted, but in the context of His sermon, Jesus has spiritual values in mind. Consider the kind of mourning mentioned in James:

> Adulterers, do you not know that friendship with the world means hostility toward God? So whoever decides to be the world's friend makes himself God's enemy. Or do you think the scripture means nothing when it says, "The spirit that God caused to live within us has an envious yearning"? But he gives greater grace. Therefore it says, "*God opposes the proud, but he gives grace to the humble.*" So submit to God. But resist the devil and he will flee from you. Draw near to God and he will draw near to you. Cleanse your hands, you sinners, and make your hearts pure, you double-minded. Grieve, mourn, and weep. Turn your laughter into mourning and your joy into despair. Humble yourselves before the Lord and he will exalt you. (James 4:4–10)

A. With what attitude is such mourning associated?

_____

_____

_____

B. When was the last time you humbled yourself before God and cried over your own sinfulness?

_____

_____

_____

_____

_____

_____

9. Matthew 5:5 says "Blessed are the meek, for they will inherit the earth." We'll discuss meekness in Saturday's devotional, but it's the attitude that comes with being in a lowly position.

A. Read Psalm 37:7–13 and notice what it has to say about meekness:

> **Psalm 37:7** Wait patiently for the Lord! Wait confidently for him! Do not fret over the apparent success of a sinner, a man who carries out wicked schemes!
>
> **37:8** Do not be angry and frustrated! Do not fret! That only leads to trouble!
>
> **37:9** Wicked men will be wiped out, but those who rely on the Lord are the ones who will possess the land.
>
> **37:10** Evil men will soon disappear; you will stare at the spot where they once were, but they will be gone.
>
> **37:11** But the oppressed will possess the land and enjoy great prosperity.
>
> **37:12** Evil men plot against the godly and viciously attack them.
>
> **37:13** The sovereign Master laughs in disgust at them, for he knows that their day is coming.

B. Compare the future of the wicked with that of the meek who hope in the Lord:

Wicked	Those Who Hope in the Lord

10. Time to take inventory. Are you poor in spirit? Mourning over your own sin? Meek? Spend time before God examining your heart and praying about what needs to change.

1. Re-read Matthew 5:6–8.

> **5:6** "Blessed are those who hunger and thirst for righteousness, for they will be satisfied.
>
> **5:7** "Blessed are the merciful, for they will be shown mercy.
>
> **5:8** "Blessed are the pure in heart, for they will see God."

2. What promise is given to those who hunger and thirst for righteousness?

_____

_____

_____

3. When was the last time you were hungry? Thirsty? In terms of intensity, what's the difference between someone who would like to be righteous and someone who hungers and thirsts for righteousness?

_____

_____

_____

_____

4. For the woman who hungers and thirsts in the way Jesus has in mind, righteousness is the passion of her life. She's totally driven by it. What would it look like for you to be passionate about righteousness? How might your schedule change? Your spending priorities? Your attitudes? What would have to be rearranged? How might you be misunderstood?

_____

_____

_____

_____

5. What promise is given to those who are merciful (see v. 7.)?

_____

_____

_____

6. Often a failure to show mercy in the face of others' sin is a failure of the imagination. That is, we cannot possibly imagine how we could do some of the "stupid things" we see others do. We may think we couldn't possibly be involved in an illicit relationship, worship the god of materialism, have a compulsion to use pornography, slander others, overeat—or be addicted to exercise! Consider a parable Jesus tells about mercy, as recorded in Luke 7:36–50.

Now one of the Pharisees asked Jesus to have dinner with him, so he went into the Pharisee's house and took his place at the table. Then when a woman of that town, who was a sinner, learned that Jesus was dining at the Pharisee's house, she brought an alabaster jar of perfumed oil. As she stood behind him at his feet, weeping, she began to wet his feet with her tears. She wiped them with her hair, kissed them, and anointed them with the perfumed oil.

Now when the Pharisee who had invited him saw this, he said to himself, "If this man were a prophet, he would know who and what kind of woman this is who is touching him, that she is a sinner."

So Jesus answered him, "Simon, I have something to say to you."

He replied, "Say it, Teacher."

"A certain creditor had two debtors; one owed him five hundred silver coins, and the other fifty. When they could not pay, he canceled the debts of both. Now which of them will love him more?"

Simon answered, "I suppose the one who had the bigger debt canceled."

Jesus said to him, "You have judged rightly." Then, turning toward the woman, he said to Simon, "Do you see this woman? I entered your house. You gave me no water for my feet, but she has wet my feet with her tears and wiped them with her hair. You gave me no kiss of greeting, but from the time I entered she has not stopped kissing my feet. You did not anoint my head with oil, but she has anointed my feet with perfumed oil. Therefore I tell you, her sins, which were many, are forgiven, thus she loved much; but the one who is forgiven little loves little." Then Jesus said to her, "Your sins are forgiven."

But those who were at the table with him began to say among themselves, "Who is this, who even forgives sins?"

He said to the woman, "Your faith has saved you; go in peace."

A significant factor in how easy it is for us to show mercy is our recognition of just how much we've been forgiven. For what have you been forgiven? (If you're honest, you'll need an extra sheet of paper.)

_____

_____

_____

_____

_____

7. To whom do you need to show mercy? How?

_____

_____

_____

8. What are the pure in heart promised (see 5:8)?

_____

_____

9. A well-known Christian who struggled with sexual compulsion said Jesus' promise that the pure in heart will see God was the truth that led to his deliverance. It wasn't enough for him to know he was hurting himself, his wife, or his testimony—as extremely important as these were. What ultimately broke his heart was the prospect of somehow not seeing God.

After David's sin with Bathsheba, he prayed to be given a pure heart (Psalm 51:10), so having a pure heart is not the same as never having sinned. Proverbs 20:9 says, "Who can say, 'I have kept my heart pure; I am clean and without sin'?"

What impurities are lurking in your heart? What false motives do you have? Confess them, mourn them, and ask God to effect a deep change in you.

THURSDAY: THE PEACEMAKERS AND THE PERSECUTED

1. Read Matthew 5:9–12.

> **5:9** "Blessed are the peacemakers, for they will be called the children of God.
>
> **5:10** "Blessed are those who are persecuted for righteousness, for the kingdom of heaven belongs to them.
>
> **5:11** "Blessed are you when people insult you and persecute you and say all kinds of evil things about you falsely on account of me. **5:12** Rejoice and be glad because your reward is great in heaven, for they persecuted the prophets before you in the same way."

2. The word "peacemaker" appears only here in the Bible. The word evokes an image of a person who sees two opposing sides and works to establish peace between them. Picture someone coming as a disinterested helper to negotiate reconciliation. Consider how Jesus was a peacemaker, coming to us when we were God's enemies and reconciling us through His death (Rom. 5:10). What promise is given to the peacemakers (see v. 9)? No doubt "peacemakers" are given such a promise because they're like God himself.

3. What are some potential pitfalls of involving a third party in a conflict?

_____

_____

_____

_____

_____

4. According to Matthew 18:15–17, when is it too early to get involved in someone else's conflict? (The bold print is the NET Bible way of flagging an Old Testament reference quoted in the New Testament.)

"If your brother sins, go and show him his fault when the two of you are alone. If he listens to you, you have regained your brother. But if he does not listen, take one or two others with you, so that *at the testimony of two or three witnesses every matter may be established.* If he refuses to listen to them, tell it to the church. If he refuses to listen to the church, treat him like a Gentile or a tax collector." (Matt. 18:15–17)

Proverbs 17:9 *says, "The one who forgives an offense seeks love, but whoever repeats a matter separates close friends." Being a peacemaker requires wisdom!*

_____

_____

5. Consider ways you can be peacemaker. Write them down. Ask the Lord to make you an instrument of His peace.

_____

_____

_____

_____

6. Why are the "persecuted because of righteousness" blessed (vv. 10, 12)?

_____

_____

_____

7. What are some forms of persecution that are unrelated to righteousness?

_____

_____

_____

_____

8. Why do you think Jesus limits the reward here to those persecuted for righteousness?

_____

_____

_____

_____

9. What are some of the forms of persecution Jesus mentions (v. 11)?

_____

_____

_____

_____

_____

10. What response are we to have when we're persecuted for the sake of righteousness? Why?

_____

_____

_____

In a *Christianity Today* editorial, David Neff noted that, unlike most American Christians, the typical Christian "lives in a developing country, speaks a non-European language, and exists under the constant threat of persecution—of murder, imprisonment, torture, or rape."[2] More Christians died for their faith in the twentieth century than in all of the previous centuries combined.[3] The current rate is about 150,000 per year.[4]

- Pray fervently for the persecuted Church.
- Ask yourself what else you can do to support your brothers and sisters who suffer.
- Locate the web sites of Christian Freedom International or Voice of the Martyrs, and look for ways to get involved.

"Open your mouth on behalf of those unable to speak, for the legal rights of all the dying." (Prov. 31:8)

[2] Chris Armstrong, "Christian History Corner: Did Eric Rudolph Act in a 'Tradition of Christian Terror'?" *Christianity Today*, online version, Week of June 9, http://www.christianitytoday.com/ct/2003/123/52.0.html, accessed January 11, 2006.

[3] Dan Wooding, "The Persecutor's Sword A Disturbing Look at Our Extended, Persecuted Family around the World," Christian History Institute, Issue #105, http://chi.gospelcom.net/GLIMPSEF/Glimpses/glmps105.shtml, accessed January 11, 2006.

[4] Richard John Neuhaus, "The Public Square," *First Things* 70, 1997, 58–74, (available online at http://www.firstthings.com/ftissues/ft9702/public.html) citing David Barrett's International Bulletin of Missionary Research.

FRIDAY: SALT AND LIGHT

1. Read Matthew 5:13–16

> You are the salt of the earth. But if salt loses its flavor, how can
> it be made salty again? It is no longer good for anything except to
> be thrown out and trampled on by people. You are the light of the
> world. A city located on a hill cannot be hidden. People do not light
> a lamp and put it under a basket but on a lampstand, and it gives
> light to all in the house. In the same way, let your light shine before
> people, so that they can see your good deeds and give honor to your
> Father in heaven. (Matt. 5:13–16)

2. When was the last time you tasted unsalted French fries? People in
Jesus' day didn't have access to the spices we have lining our grocery
store shelves, so an analogy using salt would have been particularly
effective for His audience. Some have suggested that Jesus was referring to salt as a preservative to make the point that some believers fail
to have a preserving effect on the surrounding culture. While that may
be true of many believers, nothing in this text suggests Jesus intended
such an analogy. He spoke of salt as flavoring, not as a preservative.

Matthew 5:13 is a little tricky to translate, because salt can't tech-
nically lose its saltiness; the chemical properties of salt don't change.
It's possible Jesus meant impure salt which, being exposed to sun and
rain, has had the actual saltiness drained off, leaving only sediment.
More likely, though, is the explanation that it's impossible for salt to
lose its saltiness in the same way that it's impossible for a camel to
enter the eye of a needle. Along these lines, what does verse 14 say is
impossible to hide?

___

3. Kingdom dwellers are the light of the world. What imperative does
Jesus give as a result (v. 16)? Why?

___

___

___

4. Some read verse 16 in this way: Let your light so shine before others that they may see your good works . . . and conclude that you are a genuinely nice person.

A. How can we as Christ-followers let our "lights shine" in ways that bring glory to God rather than to ourselves?

_____

_____

_____

_____

_____

B. What are some specific ways you can glorify God by being a witness to others?

_____

_____

_____

_____

5. Pray that the Lord will use your life to bring glory to himself. Ask Him for opportunities. Feel free to write your prayer below.

_____

_____

_____

_____

Scripture: "Blessed are the meek, for they will inherit the earth." (Matt. 5:5)

Rockefeller. Vanderbilt. Kennedy. These are the names of the rich and famous, leaders of dynasties—the "old money." Looking beyond U. S. shores, consider the House of Windsor or Mughal emperor Shahjahan, who built the Taj Mahal. Members of these families inherit the earth, right? They have certainly inherited some prime real estate.

Add to these old-money names all the new-money tycoons such as Oprah Winfrey, Bill Gates, and the late Sam Walton. To land my own name on the list of the world's twenty richest—of whom about half are Americans—I would need a net worth of at least $15.5 billion.

Am I materially wealthy? Not if I compare myself with these. But what if I compare my possessions against those of the world's poorest? I find that I have far more in common with those at the top than those at the bottom. You do, too.

The Bible defines a materially wealthy person as one who possesses at least one change of clothing and food for the next meal without having first to work for it. So if you're a street person with two cans of tuna and a change of clothes, you're rich. This standard of wealth was true in biblical times, and it's still true. Five hundred fifty million individuals live below the international poverty line, which is a little over $1 per day. Indeed, about half of the world's workers live on less than $2 per day. So if we were to place ourselves on a continuum from poorest to richest, those of us who collect unemployment or live on welfare still fall far closer to the high end than the low.

We can't see how rich we are, because our world sends us all sorts of messages telling us to value wealth. Vaudeville actress Sophie Tucker said, "I've been rich and I've been poor; believe me, honey—rich is better." We watch as the rich inherit the earth.

Yet Jesus said that in God's kingdom that system gets turned upside down. What we value is not what He values. There the meekest is rewarded, not the proudest, richest, or strongest.

So what *is* meekness? We don't use the word much, and when we do, we often pack it with negative nuances. We may think of Mickey Milquetoast, a lily-livered person who can't stand up to anybody—a chicken, a wimp, somebody with no backbone.

Yet that's not what Jesus had in mind. He associated meekness with humility, gentleness, and being considerate and unassuming. "Meekness" was used in Jesus' day to describe animals that were "tame," whose strength was under control. Meekness is the attitude not of the person in charge but of the slave or servant. Often we don't mind serving others—until they treat us like servants. Then we get upset. We who serve God's church often call ourselves servant-leaders, but when Paul referred to himself, he dropped the suffix and referred to himself as a bondservant.

The humble Son of Man came to serve. He washed dung off disciples' feet. Yes, Jesus—the King of the universe who will return on a white horse—described himself as meek. So if *He* was meek, how can we justify our pride?

My sister and I toured New York City recently with a group of high schoolers, and each time a limousine pulled up somewhere, we gawked to see if we recognized the person getting out. And we heard the names of famous people who own apartments overlooking Central Park. We also learned of the wealthy families who built the Empire State Building, Trump Tower, the Chrysler Building. All this the world values, but it's not what Jesus considers precious.

Go to a business seminar today, and you'll hear "how to make it to the top"; Jesus wants us to recognize that spiritually speaking, we're at the bottom. A proud person steps on others to get to the penthouse; a humble person recognizes that spiritually he or she lives in a closet in the basement. Lots of CEOs got where they are by being abrasive; a meek person is gentle. Think of Jesus—how he didn't schmooze with the top synagogue leaders. He didn't hang out with Herod. The Creator and Owner of the universe didn't namedrop with Pilate. Instead, he loved tax collectors and sinners. Think IRS agents and AIDS patients.

We have it backwards.

In the same way that we can't see how materially wealthy we are, we're often too blind to see our own truly impoverished spiritual state. If we had eyes to see, we would realize that, spiritually speaking, we're poorer than orphans combing the garbage dumps in search of not-too-rotten morsels. Only if we recognize our utterly helpless estate will we inherit the earth.

Prayer: *Heavenly Father, have mercy on me, a sinner! I fall so far short of being perfect as You are perfect. I'm proud when I should be poor in spirit. I think I'm rich when I'm poor. I remain silent rather than risk* *mockery. I accumulate material things when I should lay up treasure in heaven. Forgive me. Thank You for sending Jesus, the perfect sacrifice whose payment was sufficient to make amends for all I've done to offend You. Give me a heart that's pure, that longs to see You, that by grace exceeds the righteousness of the scribes and the Pharisees. Make me different for Your glory! In the name of your sinless Son I pray. Amen.*

For Memorization: Matthew 5:3–11

5:3 "Blessed are the poor in spirit, for the kingdom of heaven belongs to them.

5:4 "Blessed are those who mourn, for they will be comforted.

5:5 "Blessed are the meek, for they will inherit the earth.

5:6 "Blessed are those who hunger and thirst for righteousness, for they will be satisfied.

5:7 "Blessed are the merciful, for they will be shown mercy.

5:8 "Blessed are the pure in heart, for they will see God.

5:9 "Blessed are the peacemakers, for they will be called the children of God.

5:10 "Blessed are those who are persecuted for righteousness, for the kingdom of heaven belongs to them.

5:11 "Blessed are you when people insult you and persecute you and say all kinds of evil things about you falsely on account of me."

Week 2 of 6

The Law Revisited: Matthew 5:17–48

Scripture: "So then, be perfect, as your heavenly Father is perfect." (Matthew 5:48)

Have you ever bombed on a test? I mean really bombed it? I have. More than once.

In the seventh grade I took a required public speaking class. The first assignment was an impromptu speech. We were to pull a topic out of a hat and talk on the subject for three minutes. I pulled out "bones." Now if you've seen the painting "The Scream," you know how I felt. I drew a mental blank, and all I could think to say was, "Uh, bones are white. And dogs like them—they bury them. And bones are sort of porous." I sat down.

My second time up in front of the class was for a how-to speech. I had chosen as my subject, "How to make a peanut butter sandwich." The teacher required us to write out our speeches in manuscript form, and we were not allowed to veer from what we had written. This meant that if we had left out any steps, improvising at the last minute was out. We had to live with our mistakes. Unfortunately, I had left out a small detail in my speech: "Set the peanut butter and jelly jars on the table."

The result was that the person I had chosen to follow my instructions as I spoke struggled to keep the jars firmly in place under her arms as she worked to open them and then try to wield a knife. It was not supposed to be a comedy.

I wasn't used to failing so miserably, and I certainly wasn't used to doing so in front of a crowd. After that, it was at least twenty years before I had the nerve to speak in public again.

The people to whom Matthew wrote his Gospel were probably unaccustomed to failure, too. And they totally bombed it. He wrote mostly to Jews, and he had two key messages for his people: (1) your King came and you missed Him, and (2) you have the wrong idea about how to get into the kingdom of heaven.

First, the nation of Israel had missed her King because the people had wrong expectations about the Kingdom. Having been oppressed by Rome, they longed for a national deliverer who would physically reign over a temporal kingdom. They figured, "We'll show you, Rome! Everything will be wonderful when He comes. We'll overthrow you and have our own king." But the true King came to seek and to save and to serve. He had no royal scepter. Instead, He was wounded for their transgressions, bruised for their iniquities, buried with robbers.

As for how to get into the kingdom of heaven, the people had torched their chances there, too. They figured God was impressed with the happy, powerful rabbis who kept the letter of the law. But the leaders were using God to glorify themselves. They were interested mostly in earthly honor and things that are seen.

Consider the contrast Matthew shows between this group and the King they had missed:

Jewish Leaders	Jesus
Quoted rabbinical authorities	Quoted His own authority
Stressed outward conformity	Stressed inward relationship
Focused on external righteousness	Focused on the internal life
Paraded religion in public	Encouraged worship in secret
Demonstrated pride	Demonstrated humility

Before we grow too critical of the religious leaders, though, we need to see how Jesus' message still applies to those who would enter the Kingdom. All humans, not just the Jewish leaders, fall short of God's standard of perfection—a standard Jesus said was the necessary entrance pass. And knowing all have sinned and fall short of God's glory, Jesus' message is "Repent!" But most of us don't like to repent. That would require humility and brokenness and mourning over our sin. We would rather lower the standard by comparing ourselves with others and having measurable, reachable goals. If that doesn't work, we can always go buy a self-help book.

Jesus stressed that their righteousness was insufficient. They bombed the test, and so have we. It has been said that at the heart of Christianity lies a holy dread. Once we see our own sinfulness in the face of a holy God, the only thing to do is cry to God in our need: "Lord, have mercy! Christ, have mercy!" Why are our eyes so dry?

MONDAY: OVERVIEW

1. Pray for the Lord to speak to you through His Word. Then read Matthew 5:17–48.

> **Matthew 5:17** "Do not think that I have come to abolish the law or the prophets. I have not come to abolish these things but to fulfill them. **5:18** I tell you the truth, until heaven and earth pass away not the smallest letter or stroke of a letter will pass from the law until everything takes place. **5:19** So anyone who breaks one of the least of these commands and teaches others to do so will be called least in the kingdom of heaven, but whoever obeys them and teaches others to do so will be called great in the kingdom of heaven. **5:20** For I tell you, unless your righteousness goes beyond that of the experts in the law and the Pharisees, you will never enter the kingdom of heaven.
>
> **5:21** "You have heard that it was said to an older generation, *'Do not murder,'* and 'whoever murders will be subjected to judgment.' **5:22** But I say to you that anyone who is angry with a brother will be subjected to judgment. And whoever insults a brother will be brought before the council, and whoever says 'Fool' will be sent to fiery hell. **5:23** So then, if you bring your gift to the altar and there remember that your brother has something against you, **5:24** leave your gift there in front of the altar. First go and be reconciled to your brother and then come and present your gift.

5:25 Reach agreement quickly with your accuser while on the way to court, or he may hand you over to the judge, and the judge hand you over to the warden, and you will be thrown into prison. **5:26** I tell you the truth, you will never get out of there until you have paid the last penny!

5:27 "You have heard that it was said, *'Do not commit adultery.'* **5:28** But I say to you that whoever looks at a woman to desire her has already committed adultery with her in his heart. **5:29** If your right eye causes you to sin, tear it out and throw it away! It is better to lose one of your members than to have your whole body thrown into hell. **5:30** If your right hand causes you to sin, cut it off and throw it away! It is better to lose one of your members than to have your whole body go into hell.

5:31 "It was said, *'Whoever divorces his wife must give her a legal document.'* **5:32** But I say to you that everyone who divorces his wife, except for immorality, makes her commit adultery, and whoever marries a divorced woman commits adultery.

5:33 "Again, you have heard that it was said to an older generation, *'Do not break an oath, but fulfill your vows to the Lord.'* **5:34** But I say to you, do not take oaths at all—not by heaven, because it is the throne of God, **5:35** not by earth, because it is his footstool, and not by Jerusalem, because it is the city of the great King. **5:36** Do not take an oath by your head, because you are not able to make one hair white or black. **5:37** Let your word be 'Yes, yes' or 'No, no.' More than this is from the evil one.

5:38 "You have heard that it was said, *'An eye for an eye and a tooth for a tooth.'* **5:39** But I say to you, do not resist the evildoer. But whoever strikes you on the right cheek, turn the other to him as well. **5:40** And if someone wants to sue you and to take your tunic, give him your coat also. **5:41** And if anyone forces you to go one mile, go with him two. **5:42** Give to the one who asks you, and do not reject the one who wants to borrow from you.

5:43 "You have heard that it was said, *'Love your neighbor'* and 'hate your enemy.' **5:44** But I say to you, love your enemy and pray for those who persecute you, **5:45** so that you may be like your Father in heaven, since he causes the sun to rise on the evil and the good, and sends rain on the righteous and the unrighteous. **5:46** For if you love those who love you, what reward do you have? Even the tax collectors do the same, don't they? **5:47** And if you only greet your brothers, what more do you do? Even the Gentiles do the same, don't they? **5:48** So then, be perfect, as your heavenly Father is perfect.

2. Pray, asking God to transform you through interaction with His word.

3. List areas in which you fall short of God's perfect standard. Acknowledge to Him your need.

_____

_____

_____

TUESDAY: RX FOR GREATNESS

1. Re-read Matthew 5:17–20.

> **Matthew 5:17** "Do not think that I have come to abolish the law or the prophets. I have not come to abolish these things but to fulfill them. **5:18** I tell you the truth, until heaven and earth pass away not the smallest letter or stroke of a letter will pass from the law until everything takes place. **5:19** So anyone who breaks one of the least of these commands and teaches others to do so will be called least in the kingdom of heaven, but whoever obeys them and teaches others to do so will be called great in the kingdom of heaven. **5:20** For I tell you, unless your righteousness goes beyond that of the experts in the law and the Pharisees, you will never enter the kingdom of heaven.

The first step in being rightly related to God is to realize our utter need due to our sinfulness. The place we start is recognizing God is holy and that we are sinners.

2. What does Jesus say He came to do with the Law (v. 17)?

A. He has *not* come to . . .

_____

B. He *has* come to . . .

_____

Mocha on the Mount 31

3. Jesus says the tiniest letter and stroke of a pen will not pass away from the law until what has happened (v. 18)?

_____

_____

_____

4. After reading Jesus' words, do you think He thought the Pharisees' standards were too low or too high (v. 20)?

_____

_____

_____

5. How often do we hear, "Nobody's perfect"? If this is true, why do you think Jesus tells His disciples to be perfect as His Heavenly Father is perfect? Does this mean nobody can enter the Kingdom?

_____

_____

_____

6. How righteous do the people have to be to enter the Kingdom (v. 20)?

_____

_____

_____

7. Are you perfect as God is perfect (5:48)?

_____

Jesus is getting ready to tell His listeners how their leaders' standards have fallen short of what God's law requires. Jesus words could potentially sound as if He thinks the Law is wrong, so before He speaks He clarifies that He is not abolishing it or casting it aside or contradicting it in any way. Rather, He's showing them how much higher the standard is than what they thought.

WEDNESDAY: YOU HAVE HEARD, BUT . . .

1. Read Matthew 5:21–32.

> **5:21** "You have heard that it was said to an older generation, *'Do not murder*, and 'whoever murders will be subjected to judgment.' **5:22** But I say to you that anyone who is angry with a brother will be subjected to judgment. And whoever insults a brother will be brought before the council, and whoever says 'Fool' will be sent to fiery hell. **5:23** So then, if you bring your gift to the altar and there remember that your brother has something against you, **5:24** leave your gift there in front of the altar. First go and be reconciled to your brother and then come and present your gift. **5:25** Reach agreement quickly with your accuser while on the way to court, or he may hand you over to the judge, and the judge hand you over to the warden, and you will be thrown into prison. **5:26** I tell you the truth, you will never get out of there until you have paid the last penny!
>
> **5:27** "You have heard that it was said, *'Do not commit adultery.'* **5:28** But I say to you that whoever looks at a woman to desire her has already committed adultery with her in his heart. **5:29** If your right eye causes you to sin, tear it out and throw it away! It is better to lose one of your members than to have your whole body thrown into hell. **5:30** If your right hand causes you to sin, cut it off and throw it away! It is better to lose one of your members than to have your whole body go into hell.
>
> **5:31** "It was said, *'Whoever divorces his wife must give her a legal document.'* **5:32** But I say to you that everyone who divorces his wife, except for immorality, makes her commit adultery, and whoever marries a divorced woman commits adultery.

2. In the chart on the next page, list the times Jesus said, "You have heard . . . but I tell you. . . ." What are the two topics He discusses, using this approach?

What they've heard	What Jesus says

3. Do you think the average Pharisee had murdered or committed adultery?

_____

_____

4. Do you think the average Pharisee had harbored anger or lusted?

_____

5. Jesus connects the external action of murder with internal hatred and verbal abuse. He challenges any thinking that would say, "I can let anger fester; I can seethe with hatred; I can call my brother a moron. As long as I refrain from shedding his blood, I'm righteous."

A. In the Ten Commandments, what does God's Word say about killing? See Exodus 20:13 below.

Exodus 20:13 "You shall not murder."

B. Psalm 133:1 says, "Look! How good and pleasant it is when brothers live together!" The psalmist is speaking of living in family unity. This, too, was from a portion of God's Word available to the Pharisees. Which is the higher standard—to refrain from murdering or to live in unity?

_____

_____

Whereas the Pharisees' standard was the absence of something (blood), Jesus' standard is the presence of something more (reconciliation). Both are based on "the Law and the Prophets." But Jesus goes with the higher standard, placing reconciliation even above coming to God with a gift. Next He tackles adultery.

6. Jesus connects the external action of adultery with internal lust. He challenges any thinking that says, "I can use Internet porn, lust after soap opera stars, or engage in oral sex with someone I'm not married to as long as we don't have intercourse." He also challenges thinking that says, "I can divorce my spouse and marry someone I've been lusting after, and it's OK as long as we don't have sex outside of marriage."

A. What does God's law say in the Ten Commandments about committing adultery? See Exodus 20:14 below.

> **20:14** "You shall not commit adultery."

B. What else does the Old Testament say about morality? Read Proverbs 6:23–25, for example:

> **Proverbs 6:23** For the commandments are like a lamp, instruction is like a light, and rebukes of discipline are like the road leading to life,
> **6:24** by keeping you from the evil woman, from the smooth tongue of the loose woman.
> **6:25** Do not lust in your heart for her beauty, and do not let her captivate you with her alluring eyes.

_____

_____

_____

_____

_____

C. Is Jesus setting a new standard, or is He reminding them of the parts of God's law they're ignoring?

_____

_____

7. The Pharisees have chosen the letter of the law but have missed out on the intent of the law. They have focused on the externals, but Jesus goes after the internals. Notice the hyperbole He uses to show how seriously those who would enter the Kingdom should consider sin:

> "If your right eye causes you to sin, tear it out and throw it away! It is better to lose one of your members than to have your whole body thrown into hell. If your right hand causes you to sin, cut it off and throw it away! It is better to lose one of your members than to have your whole body go into hell." (Matt. 5:29–30)

A. What grudges are you harboring? Give them over to Him, and ask Him to help you pursue unity.

_____

_____

_____

B. What relationships stand in need of your attempts at reconciliation?

_____

_____

_____

C. How are you doing with lust?

_____

_____

D. God *hates* sin. What drastic action do you need to take to deal with sin in your life?

_____

_____

_____

Spend some time praying words of repentance.

Thursday: No Swearing Allowed

1. Pray for insight. Then read today's scripture (Matt. 5:33–44):

> **5:33** "Again, you have heard that it was said to an older generation, '*Do not break an oath, but fulfill your vows to the Lord.*' **5:34** But I say to you, do not take oaths at all—not by heaven, because it is the throne of God, **5:35** not by earth, because it is his footstool, and not by Jerusalem, because it is the city of the great King. **5:36** Do not take an oath by your head, because you are not able to make one hair white or black. **5:37** Let your word be 'Yes, yes' or 'No, no.' More than this is from the evil one.
>
> **5:38** "You have heard that it was said, '*An eye for an eye and a tooth for a tooth.*' **5:39** But I say to you, do not resist the evildoer. But whoever strikes you on the right cheek, turn the other to him as well. **5:40** And if someone wants to sue you and to take your tunic, give him your coat also. **5:41** And if anyone forces you to go one mile, go with him two. **5:42** Give to the one who asks you, and do not reject the one who wants to borrow from you. **5:43** "You have heard that it was said, '*Love your neighbor*' and 'hate your enemy.' **5:44** But I say to you, love your enemy and pray for those who persecute you, **5:45** so that you may be like your Father in heaven, since he causes the sun to rise on the evil and the good, and sends rain on the righteous and the unrighteous. **5:46** For if you love those who love you, what reward do you have? Even the tax collectors do the same, don't they? **5:47** And if you only greet your brothers, what more do you do? Even the Gentiles do the same, don't they? **5:48** So then, be perfect, as your heavenly Father is perfect.

2. In this section of Jesus' sermon, He focuses on two topics.

A. What topic does He cover in Matthew 5:33–37?

_____

_____

_____

B. What topic does He cover in Matthew 5:38–42?

_____

_____

_____

3. When it comes to oath-making, God himself made oaths. For example He said He would not bring another flood (Gen. 9:9–11). And the law did permit people to make oaths. Deuteronomy 10:20 says, "Revere the Lord your God, serve him, be loyal to him and take oaths only in his name." In New Testament times Paul regularly called on God as his witness. In Romans he writes "God, whom I serve with my whole heart in preaching the gospel of His Son, is my witness how constantly I remember you" (1:9). Oath-giving was intended to verify a statement's truthfulness. List some things people in our culture sometimes say or do to add credibility to their statements:

_____

_____

_____

_____

Sometimes we hear that "little white lies" are harmless, that only bold-faced lies are wrong. We may add "I promise" if our children are skeptical because of our consistent failure to follow through. Children use "I promise," too, along with "Cross my heart and hope to die."

What does Jesus say about such attempts to add credibility to our words?

_____

_____

_____

_____

4. Does your "yes" mean "yes," or does it mean "maybe"?

A. Would people who know you say they can depend on you to follow through with what you've said you'll do? Why or why not?

_____

_____

_____

B. List things you've said you'll do that you've not yet done:

_____

_____

_____

_____

C. When you R.S.V.P. that you'll attend an event, do you actually show up? Do you notify the hostess if you have a change in plans that's out of your control?

_____

_____

_____

5. Next Jesus addresses the question of justice. We do find "an eye for an eye and a tooth for a tooth" in Exodus 21, Leviticus 24, and Deuteronomy 19. The Old Testament law gives retribution guidelines to be used within a judicial system. Thus, a guy whose enemy cut off his finger was prevented from "upping the ante" by cutting off his opponent's hand. But it's important to recognize that this was legal code, not interpersonal law. Think of the "eye for eye" instructions as being somewhat like sentencing guidelines. The idea was for the punishment to fit the crime. So imagine what had happened by Jesus' day. The law intended for justice was being used to escalate conflict: " 'An eye for an eye' means I can punch you back if you hit me."

What does Jesus tell His disciples to do under the following circumstances?

A. You encounter an evil person (see 5:39).

_____

_____

_____

B. Someone strikes you on the right cheek (see 5:39).

_____

_____

_____

C. Someone wants to sue you or take your outer garment (see 5:40).

_____

_____

_____

D. Someone forces you to go a mile (see 5:41). (Soldiers in the

Roman army often commandeered citizens to carry luggage a pre-
scribed distance.)

_____

_____

_____

E. Someone wants to borrow something.

_____

_____

6. Would those who know you best describe you as generous or stingy?

_____

_____

When it comes to resisting evil, Jesus is not speaking on a judicial
level. So for example, a Christian may still serve on a police force.
Countries may still protect themselves. And when it comes to lending
to someone who asks, numerous other scriptures suggest that Jesus
probably didn't have in mind here any stranger headed for the local
bar (see Prov. 11:15; 17:18; 22:26). Rather, the idea seems to be that
Jesus won't tolerate legalism or monetary stinginess in interpersonal
relationships any more than He'll tolerate someone punching another
because he himself got hit in the face. Kingdom living is generous, not
stingy. At stake in each of Jesus' exhortations is an appeal to entrust
our personal rights to our King.

7. What are some ways in which you're tempted to seek your own
revenge?

_____

_____

_____

8. How does Jesus' emphasis on yielding personal rights differ from what the world says?

_____

_____

_____

_____

_____

FRIDAY: LIKE FATHER, LIKE SON

1. Pray, asking for insight. Then read Matthew 5:43–48.

> **Matthew 5:43** "You have heard that it was said, '*Love your neighbor*' and 'hate your enemy.' **5:44** But I say to you, love your enemy and pray for those who persecute you, **5:45** so that you may be like your Father in heaven, since he causes the sun to rise on the evil and the good, and sends rain on the righteous and the unrighteous. **5:46** For if you love those who love you, what reward do you have? Even the tax collectors do the same, don't they? **5:47** And if you only greet your brothers, what more do you do? Even the Gentiles do the same, don't they? **5:48** So then, be perfect, as your heavenly Father is perfect.

Remember the question asked of Jesus that prompted His telling the parable of the Good Samaritan? An expert in the law had asked Him, "Who is my neighbor?" (see Luke 10:29–37). The expert was looking for a loophole or a way out.

A modern-day example of trying to escape on a technicality can be seen in the example of former U.S. President Bill Clinton. Most of us remember the sordid Monica Lewinsky sex scandal that nearly brought Clinton's presidency down. When the scandal first broke to the media, the president apparently had told some aides and news anchor Jim Lehrer something to the effect that "There **is** no improper relationship." Eventually, an infamous blue dress and DNA evidence linked Mr. Clinton to compromising acts with the former White

House intern. Soon after, he was asked by a prosecutor during a grand jury testimony how he could possibly have been truthful in his claim "There is no improper relationship." The former president's evasive answer has now become a classic example of political doublespeak: "It depends on what the meaning of the word 'is' is."

Jesus didn't whip out His Webster's scroll and read an official definition of "neighbor." Instead, He told a story that made the Samaritan (the "enemy") out to be the hero. Then He asked, "Which of these was a neighbor?"

The legal expert in picking at the letter of the law had missed the spirit of the law. Here's what the law actually said: "You must not take vengeance or bear a grudge against the children of your people, but you must love your neighbor as yourself. I am the Lord" (Lev. 19:18).

The people knew this command. But the legal experts turned a command to love into a command to hate! Here's how their reasoning went: God says to love our neighbors. So that must mean we love our neighbors but hate whoever isn't our neighbor. So we love our neighbors and hate our enemies.

2. How are we supposed to treat our enemies and those who persecute us (v. 44)?

_____

_____

3. Why (vv. 45–48)?

_____

_____

4. Did Jesus practice what He preached? That is, did He love His enemies? If so, what evidence can you give to back up your conclusion?

_____

_____

_____

5. Spend some time praying that you'll be like your Heavenly Father and His Son. Write a short prayer below.

_____

_____

_____

> "For if while we were enemies we were reconciled to God through the death of his Son, how much more, since we have been reconciled, will we be saved by his life?" (Rom. 5:10)

6. After making His case for a Law that requires absolute internal righteousness, Jesus presents the standard for entry into the Kingdom: "Be perfect, therefore, as your heavenly Father is perfect." Do you meet the standard?

SATURDAY: LORD, HAVE MERCY!

Scripture: "For I tell you, unless your righteousness goes beyond that of the experts in the law and the Pharisees, you will never enter the kingdom of heaven." (Matthew 5:20)

"I don't really see why Jesus should have to die for me." The words came out of the mouth of a missionary who calls herself a Christian.

Surely she didn't just say that. She must have meant something else.

"I'm a pretty good person . . ."

Gulp.

She had said it and meant it. And her words revealed how seriously she had missed the mark.

Through the centuries the world has seen many like her. The Pharisees and teachers of the law in Jesus' day thought they were pretty good, too. And we have words for them—such as "self-righteous" and "proud."

The Pharisees seemed to have it all together. They believed the Scriptures were God's inspired Word. Their ancestors had received God's promise. And they kept the law, tithing down to the last strand of mint. But Jesus said that at their level of righteousness they weren't going to make it into the Kingdom.

Through reading Philippians 3:4–12, consider the testimony of

Paul, a Pharisee who lived at the time of Jesus:

> **Philippians 3:4** If someone thinks he has good reasons to put confidence in human credentials, I have more: **3:5** I was circumcised on the eighth day, from the people of Israel and the tribe of Benjamin, a Hebrew of Hebrews. I lived according to the law as a Pharisee. **3:6** In my zeal for God I persecuted the church. According to the righteousness stipulated in the law I was blameless. **3:7** But these assets I have come to regard as liabilities because of Christ. **3:8** More than that, I now regard all things as liabilities compared to the far greater value of knowing Christ Jesus my Lord, for whom I have suffered the loss of all things—indeed, I regard them as dung!—that I may gain Christ, **3:9** and be found in him, not because I have my own righteousness derived from the law, but because I have the righteousness that comes by way of Christ's faithfulness—a righteousness from God that is in fact based on Christ's faithfulness. **3:10** My aim is to know him, to experience the power of his resurrection, to share in his sufferings, and to be like him in his death, **3:11** and so, somehow, to attain to the resurrection from the dead. **3:12** Not that I have already attained this—that is, I have not already been perfected—but I strive to lay hold of that for which Christ Jesus also laid hold of me.

The New International Version translators of Paul's words chose to use a euphemism—"rubbish"—for what he says his own righteousness is worth. Here we see "dung" (v. 8). He actually uses the vulgar term—like our "S"-word rather than the cleaned-up ideas of "garbage" or "rubbish," which actually do have some value in a compost pile. So what's his point? Paul's own righteousness according to the Law is less than worthless. It's gross. P-*ew*! *Disgusting!*

Those who would follow God can choose one of two ways: strive for their own righteousness according to the law (and fall miserably short of His perfect standard), or have perfect righteousness credited to their account through faith in Christ, the ultimate law-keeper.

In the Sermon on the Mount, Jesus helps His readers to see their need by showing them how far they fall short of God's standard. No wonder He says, "Blessed are those who mourn, for they shall be comforted." After reading that God requires humans to be holy as He is holy, the only appropriate response is mourning accompanied by "Lord, have mercy on me—a sinner!"

We have our modern-day versions of Pharisees, don't we? They go to church. They tithe. They have Christian bumper stickers on their cars. They don't cheat on their spouses, and they've never killed anybody. On the outside they're pretty good people. The word "Christian" is no longer exclusively used of a Christ-follower. A secular publication I receive in my position as editor of a magazine informed me that it's now often used to mean "member of a right-wing political group."

Lest we point the finger anywhere other than at ourselves, however, let's consider our own bent toward legalism—assessing spirituality using an external, measurable standard. Here's a list almost guaranteed to step on our toes:

You have heard . . .	But the Bible says . . .
Tithe 10 percent of your income.	Give generously (2 Cor. 6—7).
Spiritual people don't watch TV.	If anyone lacks wisdom, let him ask of God (James 1:5).
Worship only with hymns.	. . .singing psalms, hymns, and spiritual songs with all grace in your hearts to God (Col. 3:16).
Worship only with praise songs.	See above.
Don't touch alcoholic beverages.	Whether you eat or drink, do all to the glory of God (1 Cor. 10:31).
Consume alcohol to show your liberty.	If because of [wine] your brother is hurt, you are no longer walking according to love (Rom. 14:15).
Read the Bible at least five minutes daily.	Hunger and thirst for righteousness (Matt. 5:6).
Divorce should never be considered.	Let all be harmonious, sympathetic, brotherly, kind-hearted, and humble in spirit (1 Pet. 3:8).

Spend ten minutes per day in prayer.	Pray without ceasing (1 Thess. 5:17).
A growing church is a full church.	Man looks at the outward; God looks at the heart (1 Sam. 16:7).
Smoking is bad, but french fries are OK.	Glorify God in your body (1 Cor. 6:20).
Thou shalt home school. Thou shalt private school. Thou shalt public school.	Train up a child . . .
Give to our Christian organization and we'll print your name.	Give in secret (Matt. 6:4).
Go to church.	Don't neglect gathering together (Heb. 10:25)

Are you perfect as your heavenly Father is perfect? If you're honest, you answered "no." But consider this: It was not the proud Pharisee but the tax collector who beat his chest and begged, "Lord have mercy on me—a sinner!" who went away justified—declared righteous.

God's standard is perfect holiness. But it is also perfect love. And He made a way for holiness and love to meet—at the Cross of Jesus Christ. There God's perfect standard was satisfied. Only through the perfection of Jesus Christ credited to our "account" can we ever stand rightly before God. The apostle Paul wrote to the Ephesians saying, "For by grace you are saved through faith, and this is not from yourselves, it is the gift of God; it is not from works, so that no one can boast" (Eph. 2:8–9). The main ingredient that separates Christianity from other religions is this: amazing grace!

Does that means works are unimportant? No. Paul goes on to say, "For we are his workmanship, having been created in Christ Jesus for good works that God prepared beforehand so we may do them" (2:10).

Once we recognize our utter sinfulness and acknowledge our need for Christ, the Holy Spirit indwells us. And only by the Spirit of God can our righteousness exceed that of the scribes and the Pharisees. As Jesus said, "Apart from Me, you can accomplish nothing" (John 15:15).

Prayer: *Heavenly Father, You are perfect, and I am not! I fall so far short of Your standard. So I throw myself on Your mercy, Lord. Thank You that You promise to give grace to the humble. I'm helpless, Lord, and I need Your grace! You say that You oppose the proud—help me never to think my own righteousness is worth anything but manure compared with the surpassing richness of Jesus' righteousness credited to my account. Thank You that Your son loved His enemies—of whom I was one before You reached down in mercy and called me Your own. Make my life a constant offering of gratitude for all You have done for me. In Jesus' name I pray. Amen.*

For Memorization: "Be perfect, therefore, as your heavenly Father is perfect." (Matt. 5:48)

WEEK 3 OF 6

The Secret-Filled Life: Matthew 6:1-18

Scripture: "Be careful not to display your righteousness merely to be seen by people. Otherwise you have no reward with your Father in heaven." (Matt. 6:1)

Two women deliver food to a sick woman and her family. The first brings her best dumplings and her award-winning pie. The second brings a fine roast and her mother's fabulous sponge cake. One serves out of love; the other serves so she can brag about her sacrifice. Based on the scant information I have provided so far, can you tell which one is providing food only to win human praise? Of course you can't. You would need to know more—perhaps even be omniscient.

We've all known people who have done a good work and then gone on and on about it. Most of us have done it ourselves.

Think of the person who sweeps into a meeting announcing, "Sorry I'm late; I was counseling someone with a marital crisis," rather than quietly slipping into her seat. Or the guy who complains that he hasn't slept in for three weekends because he's spent his Saturdays working at the homeless shelter. We must have the humility never to use anyone else's need as a "workshop," as Eugene Peterson puts it, "to cobble together makeshift, messianic work that inflates our importance and indispensability."

The Pharisees were guilty of that. They had an am-I-great-or-what? attitude about their good works. They drew attention to their monetary contributions so people would "ooh" and "ahh" about their generosity. They paraded their status as prayer warriors like peacocks trying to attract mates. They made sure they looked emaciated when they fasted so the fickle crowd would cheer them on.

And it made God sick.

He wants us to perform our good works in private—as my grandmother did when my aunt died. School bills had eaten up all our discretionary income, and then we got the bad news. I made the Dallas-to-Portland flight with only a few dollars in my purse. But to my surprise, after the service I discovered a crisp bill in my coat pocket. I was sure it hadn't been there a few hours earlier. My brother, upon seeing my face when I found it, whispered, "I saw Grama slip it in there when she thought nobody was looking."

That is a picture of how Jesus would have us handle acts of righteousness. No bragging. No holding the backs of our hands to our foreheads, going on about how we'll recover from the inconvenience. No punching our own martyr cards. Only stealth kindnesses that tangibly demonstrate belief in our omniscient God.

There's a down side to doing works in secret, of course. People might think we're failing to pull our weight if we keep them in the dark about all we've done. They might misunderstand us.

Cha-ching. Hear the award accumulating in the heavenly cash register? Jesus was misunderstood all the time, so we're in great company.

Worse yet, someone else might take credit for what we've done. It takes a lot of maturity to stand by and watch while someone accepts applause he or she doesn't deserve. It's one thing for nobody to receive praise; it's much harder when the wrong person grabs the limelight.

When these things happen, it's helpful to know that one of God's names is *El Roi.*

Back in Genesis when Sarai mistreated Hagar, Hagar fled. Then the angel of the Lord appeared to her near a spring in the desert and asked, "Servant of Sarai, where have you come from, and where are you going?"

"I'm running away from my mistress, Sarai," she answered.

"Go back and submit to her. I will so increase your descendants that they will be too numerous to count. You are now with child and you will have a son. You shall name him Ishmael—God hears—for the Lord has heard of your misery."

After this interchange, Hagar calls the Lord "El Roi"—the God who sees.

In addition to the spiritual benefit we receive from doing righteous deeds, Jesus adds a bonus: "Your heavenly Father who sees in secret will reward you." So we have a choice. We can take our payback now in the form of others' fleeting praise, or we can delay gratification for a day when our treasures laid up in heaven will pay eternal dividends from the hand of a benevolent multi-zillionaire Father.

You do the math.

Monday: Overview

1. Ask the Lord to change you through interaction with His Word. Then read this week's scripture, Matthew 6:1–18.

> **Matthew 6:1** "Be careful not to display your righteousness merely to be seen by people. Otherwise you have no reward with your Father in heaven. **6:2** Thus whenever you do charitable giving, do not blow a trumpet before you, as the hypocrites do in synagogues and on streets so that people will praise them. I tell you the truth, they have their reward. **6:3** But when you do your giving, do not let your left hand know what your right hand is doing, **6:4** so that your gift may be in secret. And your Father, who sees in secret, will reward you.
>
> **6:5** "Whenever you pray, do not be like the hypocrites, because they love to pray while standing in synagogues and on street corners so that people can see them. Truly I say to you, they have their reward. **6:6** But whenever you pray, go into your room, close the door, and pray to your Father in secret. And your Father, who sees in secret, will reward you. **6:7** When you pray, do not babble repetitiously like the Gentiles, because they think that by their many words they will be heard. **6:8** Do not be like them, for your Father knows what you need before you ask him. **6:9** So pray this way: Our Father in heaven, may your name be honored,
>
> **6:10** may your kingdom come, may your will be done on earth as it is in heaven.

6:11 Give us today our daily bread,

6:12 and forgive us our debts, as we ourselves have forgiven our debtors.

6:13 And do not lead us into temptation, but deliver us from the evil one.

6:14 "For if you forgive others their sins, your heavenly Father will also forgive you. **6:15** But if you do not forgive others, your Father will not forgive you your sins.

6:16 "When you fast, do not look sullen like the hypocrites, for they make their faces unattractive so that people will see them fasting. I tell you the truth, they have their reward. **6:17** When you fast, put oil on your head and wash your face, **6:18** so that it will not be obvious to others when you are fasting, but only to your Father who is in secret. And your Father, who sees in secret, will reward you.

2. What are some forms of human approval people receive from doing good works?

_____

_____

_____

_____

_____

3. List ways in which works of Christian charity are sometimes made public.

_____

_____

_____

_____

_____

4. Ask the Lord to show you some creative ways to keep your good works anonymous. List them here:

_____

_____

_____

TUESDAY: SLEIGHT OF HAND

1. Pray for insight, and then read Matthew 6:1–4.

> **6:1** "Be careful not to display your righteousness merely to be seen by people. Otherwise you have no reward with your Father in heaven. **6:2** Thus whenever you do charitable giving, do not blow a trumpet before you, as the hypocrites do in synagogues and on streets so that people will praise them. I tell you the truth, they have their reward. **6:3** But when you do your giving, do not let your left hand know what your right hand is doing, **6:4** so that your gift may be in secret. And your Father, who sees in secret, will reward you.

2. Note that Jesus does not say "if" you give to the needy, but "when." What are some of the forms neediness takes?

_____

_____

_____

3. List ways you can give to others in need. Think beyond financial help to additional ways of ministering God's grace.

_____

_____

_____

4. One way to give in secret is to pray for others. Pray for those in need, beginning with yourself and your family. List those for whom you'll pray right now:

_____

_____

_____

_____

5. Notice that Jesus doesn't say the *reason* to give is so you'll receive a reward. The heavenly reward is a natural end result. Remember in an earlier study we read that we should live in such a way that people will see our works and glorify our Father. Are you giving God the glory, or are you hoarding praise for yourself?

_____

_____

_____

WEDNESDAY: THE CLOSET PRAY-ER

1. Ask God to give you insight into the text. Then read Matthew 6:5–8.

> **Matthew 6:5** "Whenever you pray, do not be like the hypocrites, because they love to pray while standing in synagogues and on street corners so that people can see them. Truly I say to you, they have their reward. **6:6** But whenever you pray, go into your room, close the door, and pray to your Father in secret. And your Father, who sees in secret, will reward you. **6:7** When you pray, do not babble repetitiously like the Gentiles, because they think that by their many words they will be heard. **6:8** Do not be like them, for your Father knows what you need before you ask him.

2. Notice that again Jesus does not say "if" but "when" you pray. Describe your prayer life:

_____

_____

_____

3. Do you pray more frequently and/or more enthusiastically in a crowd than in private? Do you ever change how you pray in order to gain others' approval?

_____

_____

_____

4. What two instructions does Jesus give about prayer (vv. 6–7)?

_____

_____

_____

5. Where do you find is the best place to pray? Where is your prayer closet?

_____

_____

_____

6. Jesus refers to pagans babbling in prayer, using endless repetition. He's probably speaking of those who believed in many gods and offered their petitions to each in order to cover all the bases. Then pagans would repeat themselves in hopes of increasing their odds of

being heard. How is prayer to our heavenly Father different from prayer to false gods?

_____

_____

_____

7. Why does Jesus say His followers should not babble in repetition (see v. 8)? Do you trust Him to know your needs?

_____

_____

_____

THURSDAY: THE PRAYER OF JESUS

1. Ironically, though Jesus has just told His followers to avoid vain repetition, the sample prayer He offered is probably the most repeated prayer in history. The question is not whether we should pray it, but how we do so. Read it attentively and prayerfully:

Our Father, who art in heaven, hallowed be Thy name.
Thy kingdom come, Thy will be done on earth as it is in heaven.
Give us this day our daily bread,
And forgive us our trespasses, as we forgive those who trespass against us.
And lead us not into temptation, but deliver us from evil.
For Thine is the kingdom, and the power, and the glory forever. Amen.

2. Though Jesus has told His followers to pray in secret, clearly He intends for them to sometimes pray with others. Circle the first word of His model prayer?

6:9 So pray this way: Our Father in heaven, may your name be honored,

6:10 may your kingdom come, may your will be done on earth as it is in heaven.

6:11 Give us today our daily bread,

6:12 and forgive us our debts, as we ourselves have forgiven our debtors.

6:13 And do not lead us into temptation, but deliver us from the evil one.

3. Three chapters earlier, we read where Jesus told the Pharisees and Sadducees, "Do not think you can say to yourselves, 'We have Abraham as our *father* . . .' " (italics mine). Up to this point, God's people recognized Abraham as their father. They worshiped God as the Creator and Lord but never as "our Father." Today we're so familiar with the teaching about God as heavenly Father that we lack the understanding the disciples had of awe, reverence, and holy fear. What are the first three requests Jesus offers to the Father (vv. 9–10), and what do they have in common?

_____

_____

_____

4. What are the next three requests Jesus makes? (See vv. 11–13.)

_____

_____

_____

5. Jesus instructs His disciples to pray, "Give us this day our daily bread." In week one, we defined a materially wealthy person as one who possesses a change of clothing and food for the next meal before having to earn it first. So we're somewhat removed from the degree of dependence exhibited in Jesus' prayer for daily bread, since most of us have canisters of flour, sugar, rice, and barley; six cans of soup; two boxes of crackers; four jars of fruit; several cans of tomato paste; and a box of Girl Scout cookies—on the second shelf alone. One of the writers of Proverbs prayed this:

Remove falsehood and lies far from me; do not give me poverty or riches, feed me with my allotted bread, lest I become satisfied and act deceptively and say, "Who is the Lord?" or lest I become poor and steal and harm the name of my God (Prov. 30:8–9).

According to this writer, what danger is inherent in having the kind of abundance we enjoy?

_____

_____

_____

_____

6. "Forgive us our sins as we forgive those who sin against us." Forgiving others is great—in theory. But what happens when I find out someone tempted my husband to cheat? Or told lies about me? Or stole my identity? When people sin against us, the choice to grant forgiveness can be among the most difficult we make. The word "as" introduces a comparison. So in Jesus' prayer, what connection does He make between God's forgiving us and our forgiving others?

_____

_____

_____

_____

7. Jesus prays, "Do not lead us into temptation, but deliver us from evil." This is not to suggest God leads people into temptation. (James 1:13 says God does not tempt anyone.) The phrase is a rhetorical way of asking for victory over sin. Spend some time praying for God to give you success in areas where you habitually give in to temptation.

8. Jesus ends with "For if you forgive men when they sin against you, your heavenly Father will also forgive you. But if you do not forgive

men their sins, your Father will not forgive your sins." What is the cause-effect relationship between what you give and what you receive? Why do you think this is so?

_____

_____

_____

FRIDAY: FAST, NOT FURIOUS

1. Ask for God to speak to you through His Word. Then read today's verses:

> **Matthew 6:16–18:** "When you fast, do not look sullen like the hypocrites, for they make their faces unattractive so that people will see them fasting. I tell you the truth, they have their reward. **6:17** When you fast, put oil on your head and wash your face, **6:18** so that it will not be obvious to others when you are fasting, but only to your Father who is in secret. And your Father, who sees in secret, will reward you."

2. Note the first word in verse 16. Why do you think Jesus said "when" rather than "if"?

_____

_____

_____

3. Do you ever fast? Why or why not? (Some have legitimate medical reasons for not fasting.)

_____

_____

_____

4. Many associate fasting with legalism, but it doesn't have to be that way any more than giving to the needy or praying are the activities of legalists. What are some reasons—good, neutral, and bad—that people have for fasting today?

_____

_____

_____

5. What instruction does Jesus give for how His disciples should fast?

_____

_____

_____

6. In the next week, plan to fast at least one meal if you have no medical reason keeping you from doing so. As you give up something, meditate on the sacrifices Jesus made to dwell among us and to die for us. What meal(s) on what day can you fast? How can you make fasting part of your routine?

_____

_____

_____

"Fasting is the act of temporarily giving up something that is very important to us in order that we may use the time normally given to that thing for prayer and reflection upon the pain of the temporary 'sacrifice' to better understand the mystery and meaning of Christ's passion and sacrifice for us. . . . We pray for those who are hungry every day, for those who never know the privilege of a fast because they are forced to starve."[5]

[5] Rueben P. Job and Norman Shawchuck, *A Guide to Prayer* (Nashville: The Upper Room, 1983), 9.

For Memorization: "For if you forgive others their sins, your heavenly Father will also forgive you. But if you do not forgive others, your Father will not forgive you your sins." (Matt. 6:14–15)

We had slaved to create an Easter production. The props had been painted, the music memorized and mastered, the costumes designed. Having finally made it to dress rehearsal, we added stage makeup.

As one of the townspeople in the production, I had two reasons for bouncing on the tips of my toes. First, I had written the script. Second, the choir director had chosen my husband to play the part of Jesus. Watching my own words come to life was the closest thing to creating *ex nihilo* I'd ever get. And seeing my husband top it off by bringing his talent to the drama was better than a three-layer chocolate cake.

Nearly everyone knows how the Easter story turns out. So we added a sub-plot about a lame girl whose family kept trying to take her to Jesus, but they kept arriving too late. Her father's character sang a moving rendition of "When Answers Aren't Enough, There Is Jesus."

And in the middle of his solo it happened—a man came running down the center aisle yelling like a crazy person. He was wearing a cave-man-like outfit, and his hair was flying everywhere. Picture "Albert Einstein meets Fred Flintstone."

My husband, playing Jesus, looked stunned. I stood there with my mouth hanging open, too. Then one of the directors quickly announced that a demon-possessed man was being added at the last minute. "At this point, we'll need Jesus to heal him," the director said.

I was furious.

The mood of the solo would be interrupted, the blocking my husband had worked hard to memorize had been changed, and the new guy looked more like someone from a bad skit than someone needing healing. My drama had been ruined! And my pride was hurt—people would see it and think I had put that silly scene in there.

After we finished rehearsing, I went to the person who had made the last-minute decision and pleaded with him to drop the new vignette. But he set his jaw and told me to get over it.

So I took a walk.

I knew that if I went back to the choir room, my friends would gather round me and say how unreasonable it all was, but that was not the best option for church unity. If I went and commiserated with my husband, I would only make it more difficult for him to have a good attitude, considering my frame of mind. So I went upstairs and found some deserted steps. Then I prayed, "Lord, I'm not sure I can even be in this production considering how angry I am. Should I just quietly go home? How am I going to handle this?"

Before long, the church secretary, a wise, godly woman who can keep a confidence, came along and saw my tear-soaked costume. She sat on the step next to me and rested a hand on my back. I proceeded to tell her what had happened. "What do you think I should do?" I asked.

She sighed and shook her head. "This is going to be hard, but . . . go down there with the best attitude you can muster, and perform your heart out as a sacrifice to Jesus. Offer Him all your bad feelings as a willing offering."

Gulp.

Even though I sensed that's exactly what the Spirit was prompting me to do, it took all the strength I had plus some supernatural empowering to follow her recommendation. I didn't want to forgive that director. But I also didn't want God refusing to forgive me. In the Sermon on the Mount, Jesus had made it clear that God's forgiveness of my sins is linked with my forgiveness of others. I'm not sure exactly how that works, but I knew what I needed to do. So I took a deep breath and told God, "OK, I forgive him."

Then something remarkable happened the next time I stood on stage. I saw things differently. I watched my husband as Jesus bearing a cross. He had ketchup on his back, but it looked like blood, and it tore me up to envision someone I love so much being treated so harshly. And I realized, "I did that to the beloved Jesus." He bore the cross for me. I fell so far short of God's holy standard that I had to have a Savior. And He took my place. He gave up his life to forgive my sins."

All I had really sacrificed to forgive was releasing my pride, letting go of a grudge, and singing on stage when I didn't feel like it. Big whoop. What had Jesus done to show He forgave? He spent thirty-some years minus the adoration of angels, and He endured mocking, spitting, nakedness, whipping, and nails in His hands and feet. And as if that weren't enough, He endured the wrath of His Father—the one whose fellowship He had enjoyed since eternity past. I was the one who really deserved that wrath for falling so far short of His standard of holiness.

No wonder it offends God when we refuse to forgive. Nothing anyone does to us is worthy of being compared to what we've done to Him. If He can forgive us to the point of death, why can't we forgive when it costs us so much less?

Recently I read in the news about a man who murdered a nine-year-old girl. The girl's father said of the criminal, "I hope he burns in hell." Her grandfather said, "May God have mercy on his soul."

I identified with the former. Jesus calls us to the latter.

Prayer: *Heavenly Father, Thank You for forgiving my sins. Because I'm such a stranger to Your holiness, I have trouble grasping how deeply my sinfulness offends You. Give me the eyes to see how far short I fall of Your perfect standard so I might be filled with grace for others who offend both You and me. Give me the heart to forgive those who have wronged me, not so people will comment on what a great person I am, but because it's the least I can do considering the price paid for me. Make me into that child who looks just like her Father. In the name of Your precious Son I pray. Amen.*

For Memorization: "Be careful not to display your righteousness merely to be seen by people. Otherwise you have no reward with your Father in heaven." (Matt. 6:1)

Week 4 of 6

About Storage: Matthew 6:19–34

Scripture: "Do not accumulate for yourselves treasures on earth, where moth and rust destroy, and where thieves break in and steal." (Matt. 6:19)

Several months ago as I was paying my credit card bill, I noticed two unfamiliar charges made in a neighboring city. They totaled nearly $200. I called my husband to ask if he recognized them, but he reminded me he was on a business trip during the two dates the charges were made.

The only time our cards had left our possession was when we had paid for food at restaurants. Fortunately we caught the problem quickly, the amount wasn't significant, and the credit card company covered the loss. (Later we were notified that a group of thieves at our gas station had installed a machine that picked up numbers off credit cards; the thieves are now doing time.)

The incident served as a good reminder that despite all our efforts to protect, whether with shredders or insurance policies or homeland security, we can't hang on to any of it.

Consider what was taken in Lindale, Texas. When the county constable got a call reporting a stolen house, he asked, "Was it a trailer?" The real estate company rep insisted, "No, it's a brick house."

Apparently thieves spent three months stripping a residence of its boards and shingles, dismantling it, and leaving behind only a pile of trash. In plain view of the neighbors—some of whom even waved—two men stole a house and sold it for drugs.

Along those lines, can you guess what each of the following items has in common?

- The Helen Keller archives
- Numerous pieces of artwork and sculpture on display
- Over 40,000 negatives of President John F. Kennedy

If you said they were all destroyed on September 11, 2001, along with the twin towers in New York City, you're right. Add to that the losses sustained by hundreds of Chase Manhattan Bank customers who stored precious possessions in safe deposit boxes, which banks don't insure. And that's not even counting the most priceless loss—more than 2,700 lives.

The world is not a safe place.

Picture any natural disaster, whether tsunami, earthquake, tornado, hurricane, mudslide, volcano, flood, or blizzard, and at the end you have untold loss. Countless lives, homes, businesses and entire communities are destroyed every day.

Jesus noted that moth and rust and thieves threaten our earthly possessions. Losses caused by the first two involve natural processes. The latter happens due to sin. But either way despite our best efforts, we can't control everything that happens.

That is, unless we send it on ahead. We do have some control about what gets credited to our eternal bank account, where nothing can destroy what we've laid aside. By embracing a system that values the immaterial over the material, we guarantee for ourselves lasting treasure.

On this earth eventually it's all going to burn—which reminds me of the words I heard once from Gene Getz, a Dallas pastor whose church was torched by an arsonist. Upon returning to his office after it was destroyed, he found that only one thing had endured. In the center of his floor lay a copy of a book he had written. Its pages were black and curled, but he could still read the title: *A Biblical Theology of Material Possessions.*

1. Pray for insight into the text. Then read Matthew 6:19–34.

Matthew 6:19 "Do not accumulate for yourselves treasures on earth, where moth and rust destroy and where thieves break in and steal. **6:20** But accumulate for yourselves treasures in heaven, where moth and rust do not destroy, and thieves do not break in and steal. **6:21** For where your treasure is, there your heart will be also.

6:22 "The eye is the lamp of the body. If then your eye is healthy, your whole body will be full of light. **6:23** But if your eye is diseased, your whole body will be full of darkness. If then the light in you is darkness, how great is the darkness!

6:24 "No one can serve two masters, for either he will hate the one and love the other, or he will be devoted to the one and despise the other. You cannot serve God and money.

6:25 "Therefore I tell you, do not worry about your life, what you will eat or drink, or about your body, what you will wear. Isn't there more to life than food and more to the body than clothing? **6:26** Look at the birds in the sky: They do not sow, or reap, or gather into barns, yet your heavenly Father feeds them. Aren't you more valuable than they are? **6:27** And which of you by worrying can add even one hour to his life? **6:28** Why do you worry about clothing? Think about how the flowers of the field grow; they do not work or spin. **6:29** Yet I tell you that not even Solomon in all his glory was clothed like one of these! **6:30** And if this is how God clothes the wild grass, which is here today and tomorrow is tossed into the fire to heat the oven, won't he clothe you even more, you people of little faith? **6:31** So then, don't worry saying, 'What will we eat?' or 'What will we drink?' or 'What will we wear?' **6:32** For the unconverted pursue these things, and your heavenly Father knows that you need them. **6:33** But above all pursue his kingdom and righteousness, and all these things will be given to you as well. **6:34** So then, do not worry about tomorrow, for tomorrow will worry about itself. Today has enough trouble of its own."

2. Jesus gives a "do" and a "don't" relating to possessions (verses 19–20). What are they?

_____

_____

_____

_____

_____

3. If Jesus were to appear and take inventory of your possessions, would He find more laid up on earth or more in heaven? Do you need to make some changes in order to have a biblical "bottom line"? If so, what?

_____

_____

_____

_____

TUESDAY: STASHING HIDDEN TREASURE

1. Ask God to change your life to bring it in line with Kingdom values. Then read today's verses:

> **Matthew 6:19** "Do not accumulate for yourselves treasures on earth, where moth and rust destroy and where thieves break in and steal. **6:20** But accumulate for yourselves treasures in heaven, where moth and rust do not destroy, and thieves do not break in and steal. **6:21** For where your treasure is, there your heart will be also."

2. What are the three means Jesus lists through which property gets destroyed (v. 19)?

_____

_____

_____

_____

3. List at least five other ways in which property can be destroyed.

_____

_____

_____

_____

_____

4. Name some times when your own possessions have been destroyed.

_____

_____

_____

_____

5. How did you feel?

_____

_____

_____

6. List some of the means we employ for assuring the security of our possessions.

_____

_____

7. What is true of heavenly possessions that's not true of earthly possessions (v. 20)?

_____

_____

_____

_____

8. What does Jesus say is a result of laying up treasure in heaven instead of earth (v. 21)? Notice that He says our hearts follow our possessions, rather than the other way around. In other words, we develop passion for things in which we've already invested.

_____

_____

_____

_____

WEDNESDAY: THE EYES HAVE IT

1. Pray for insight. Then meditate on today's reading:

> **6:22** "The eye is the lamp of the body. If then your eye is healthy, your whole body will be full of light. **6:23** But if your eye is diseased, your whole body will be full of darkness. If then the light in you is darkness, how great is the darkness!
>
> **6:24** "No one can serve two masters, for either he will hate the one and love the other, or he will be devoted to the one and despise the other. You cannot serve God and money.

6:25 "Therefore I tell you, do not worry about your life, what you will eat or drink, or about your body, what you will wear. Isn't there more to life than food and more to the body than clothing?

2. The phrase "The eye is the lamp of the body" may at first be a little difficult to grasp. To understand what Jesus is talking about, go back and observe Matthew 6:19–21. What topic was being discussed in these verses (which fall right before the section about the eye being the lamp)?

_____

_____

_____

_____

3. Now look at the verse that follows the discussion about the eye. What's the topic at hand in Matthew 6:24?

_____

_____

_____

_____

4. Some think the verses for today's reading mean "You can tell somebody's a Christian by merely looking at the joy in his or her eyes." Yet when we look at the context, it seems best to understand Jesus' words about the eyes as relating to a continuing discussion about Kingdom values. Three metaphors are employed in the discussion: treasure, light, and servanthood. The Greek word for "good" in the phrase "if your eyes are good" is the same word translators used about two thousand years ago in the Hebrew-to-Greek translation to denote singleness of purpose or undivided loyalty. We use the word "eye" similarly when we say "he has his eye on the prize." The section we're exploring this week emphasizes committed loyalty to eternal values.

A. What do you most treasure?

_____

_____

_____

_____

B. What are your top priorities?

_____

_____

_____

_____

C. Whom do you serve—God or things? Give evidence.

_____

_____

_____

_____

5. What does Jesus say is a major problem with having two masters (vv. 24–25)?

_____

_____

_____

_____

6. What two masters does Jesus say His disciples cannot serve at the same time?

_____

_____

_____

_____

7. What are some ways people demonstrate that they're enslaved to money?

_____

_____

_____

_____

8. List evidences that you've been affected by materialism.

_____

_____

_____

9. What changes do you need to make to demonstrate a shift in priorities?

_____

_____

_____

_____

_____

THURSDAY: LILY LABOR?

1. Read this week's scripture after praying for insight:

> **Matthew 6:25** "Therefore I tell you, do not worry about your life, what you will eat or drink, or about your body, what you will wear. Isn't there more to life than food and more to the body than clothing? **6:26** Look at the birds in the sky: They do not sow, or reap, or gather into barns, yet your heavenly Father feeds them. Aren't you more valuable than they are? **6:27** And which of you by worrying can add even one hour to his life? **6:28** Why do you worry about clothing? Think about how the flowers of the field grow; they do not work or spin. **6:29** Yet I tell you that not even Solomon in all his glory was clothed like one of these! **6:30** And if this is how God clothes the wild grass, which is here today and tomorrow is tossed into the fire to heat the oven, won't he clothe you even more, you people of little faith?

2. What is the first word in verse 25?

_____

3. An important directive of biblical interpretation is this: Any time you find the word "therefore," find out what it's there for. This is the conclusion of an argument. What topic was Jesus discussing, as recorded in the preceding verses?

4. What questions did Jesus raise (see v. 25)? What are the obvious answers?

_____

_____

5. What two broad categories did Jesus include for what His followers were not to worry about?

_____

_____

_____

_____

6. In each of these categories He gave specific examples. What were they?

_____

_____

_____

_____

7. What were Jesus' disciples to learn from the birds (v. 26)?

_____

_____

_____

_____

_____

8. What were Jesus' disciples supposed to learn from the lilies (vv. 28–30)?

_____

_____

9. Between giving two examples from nature, Jesus asked a question, in verse 27. What is the answer, and what is His point?

_____

_____

_____

_____

10. Take inventory. How are you doing with the following?

A. Worrying about buying groceries

_____

_____

_____

B. Worry about buying clothing

_____

_____

_____

C. Stockpiling food and clothing

_____

_____

_____

D. Worrying about tomorrow

_____

_____

_____

FRIDAY: FIRST THINGS FIRST

1. Prayerfully read the verses for today:

> **Matthew 6:31** So then, don't worry saying, 'What will we eat?' or 'What will we drink?' or 'What will we wear?' **6:32** For the unconverted pursue these things, and your heavenly Father knows that you need them. **6:33** But above all pursue his kingdom and righteousness, and all these things will be given to you as well. **6:34** So then, do not worry about tomorrow, for tomorrow will worry about itself. Today has enough trouble of its own.

2. Do you think or talk more about what you will eat, drink, and wear than you do about eternal pursuits?

_____

_____

_____

_____

3. What two reasons did Jesus give for why His disciples should not worry about food, drink, and clothing (see verse 32)?

_____

_____

_____

4. Jesus gave a "don't" (v. 31) and a "do" (v. 33) in this section of His sermon. What were they?

_____

_____

_____

5. What promise was given as recorded in verse 33?

_____

_____

_____

6. What two reasons did Jesus give for why we should not worry about tomorrow (v. 34)? Notice Jesus' emphasis in His sermon on taking one day at a time. Think of the Lord's Prayer: "Give us *this day* our *daily* bread."

_____

_____

_____

7. After considering all Jesus has to say about what our value system should look like, list one or more changes you can make this week. Pray about what God would have you do in the long term.

_____

_____

_____

_____

SATURDAY: BLOUSE THEOLOGY

Scripture: "Your will be done on earth as it is in heaven" (Matt. 6:10)

I have a friend who shares tongue-in-cheek her theory about how to know God's will when shopping. It's called "blouse theology": "If I find a blouse I love, it might be God's will; if it goes on sale, it's definitely God's will."

Often we connect God's will with our need for guidance in making decisions, big and little. And there's certainly an element of truth in that. We do need God to show us the right path in all things. Should I marry this person? Should I change jobs? Should we relocate? Should I buy this car? Lord, what do You want me to do?

Sometimes, though, we lose sight of the fact that God is less concerned with what blouse I buy than whether I'm generous. His priority is on who He wants us to *be*. Consider what we've learned of God's will from the portions of Scripture we've explored so far:

It's God's will that I . . .
- am poor in spirit
- mourn over my sin
- exhibit meekness
- hunger and thirst for righteousness
- show mercy
- make peace
- bless those who persecute me
- rejoice in persecution
- let my light shine so God is glorified
- keep and teach all His commandments
- have righteousness that surpasses that of the Pharisees
- refrain from anger
- avoid name-calling
- initiate reconciliation
- make friends with my legal opponent
- don't lust
- deal harshly with sin
- honor my marriage covenant
- keep my word
- return evil with good
- love and pray for my enemies

- am perfect as He is perfect
- practice my righteousness in secret
- forgive others
- give to the needy
- pray
- fast
- lay up my treasures in heaven, not on earth

I don't know about you, but that's enough to keep me occupied for a while!

Who should we be becoming? That's the question most of Scripture answers when the subject of "God's will" comes up. Paul wrote to the Thessalonians, "This is the will of God—your sanctification" (1 Thess. 4:3). My college years might have started with a prayer of "Where do You want me to go?" but I should have devoted much more attention to asking, "Now that I'm here, how can I serve You on this campus for Your glory?"

Are you struggling to know God's will? Remember that He's revealed most of it already. Be holy. Don't lust. Return evil with good. Practice your righteousness in secret. Be humble. Mourn over your sin. Hunger and thirst for righteousness. As you wait for His answer on "what," remember to continue being *who* He wants you to be.

The cries of those less fortunate ring in our ears. As we become the Christ-followers He wants us to be, we may need to put off replacing the car to give more funds to a ministry serving AIDS patients. Or we may need to forego dinners out to help feed the hungry. Or pass up even a sale-marked blouse to help a single mom needing to clothe her kids. Now *that's* "blouse theology"!

Prayer: *Heavenly Father, thank You that You promise to clothe me, since I'm worth so much more to You than a field lily. And thank You that You've always fed me, clothed me, and provided for my every need. Forgive me for worrying about tomorrow when today has enough difficulty. Give me a proper perspective on material things. Help me rearrange my priorities to reflect those of a Kingdom-dweller. Thank You for the reminder that it'll all burn up in the end unless I've sent it ahead for safekeeping in Your vaults. Help me to live as though I believe that. And thank You that You know my needs before I ask. In Jesus' name I pray. Amen.*

For Memorization: "But accumulate for yourselves treasures in heaven, where moth and rust do not destroy, and thieves do not break in and steal. For where your treasure is, there your heart will be also." (Matt. 6:20–21)

WEEK 5 OF 6

Sticking to a Single Standard: Matthew 7:1–12

Scripture: "Or how can you say to your brother, 'Let me remove the speck from your eye,' while there is a beam in your own?" (Matt. 7:4)

Our women's Bible study was going through the Sermon on the Mount, and the leaders had met to discuss how we could illustrate sections of it through drama or video clips. We came to the part where Jesus says, "How can you say to your brother, 'Let me take the speck out of your eye, when all the time there is a plank in your own eye?'" and my friend, Sheila, piped up. "I have a graphic illustration of this verse if you'd like to use it," she said. "It's from footage of me on TV—when I was a contestant on *Wheel of Fortune*."

She certainly had our attention. Even though she was my neighbor and a close friend, I had no idea she had ever been on TV, let alone met Vanna White.

Shelia told us how she had won round after round, winning herself a trip to Europe and a red convertible. We asked if she was serious.

81

A few days later I sat in her living room and watched the clip for myself. It was obviously old, as her Farrah Fawcett haircut and 1980s wardrobe indicated. But sure enough, there she was, celebrating with Pat Sajak and Vanna.

As I watched, I saw why she thought the clip would serve as a good illustration of Jesus' words. And I appreciated her humility in offering herself as an example of what *not* to do.

She was so excited, bouncing and screaming with her mouth wide open half the time. Then Pat Sajak called her husband out of the crowd to come down and celebrate with her. Ray ran down, hugged Sheila, and shook hands with Pat and Vanna while the streamers swirled around them all. Then I saw the part Sheila had told us about. She leaned toward Ray and whispered something in his ear. He gave her a funny look, and then they resumed celebrating.

"I was telling him to shut his mouth," she explained. "I thought it was hanging open so far that people could see his fillings. Not until I saw the footage after we returned home did I realize that my own mouth would have caught a lot more flies than his."

The way she saw it, Ray had had a piece of sawdust in his eye while she had a board in her own.

The following week we showed Sheila's video. She told her story and in doing so endeared herself to every woman present. Who of us has not been the "pot calling the kettle black "? It's so easy to be critical of others when we ourselves are far worse. We hate it when someone cuts us off in traffic, but we justify sliding in front of another car "just this once" when we're late for an appointment. We loathe it when people share our private business, but then we say stuff like "Pray for Julie—she and her husband are having financial difficulties." An example from my own experience as a parent would include the time I yelled at my daughter with "Stop yelling at me!"

Often we pride ourselves in being critical thinkers—discerning the rightness or wrongness of all we hear—when, truth be told, we're really little more than fault-finding critics. The human ability to deceive oneself is deeply ingrained.

On the flip side, people may read Jesus' words "Do not judge, or you too will be judged," and take Him to mean we're never to say anything that could be construed as negative. They may see a friend engage in ticket-scalping and assume they're supposed to remain quiet because no one made them judge and jury. Or they may hear someone who claims to be a professing believer saying she's a lesbian and proud of it (as has happened to me), and assume objecting is intolerant.

"You hypocrite," He says. "*First* take the plank out of your own eye, and *then* you will see clearly to remove the speck from your brother's eye" (emphasis added). Jesus does expect us to remove the speck—to speak up about what's wrong—once we can see clearly. He just expects us to live up to the same standards we have for others. It's all too easy to have a double standard—a high standard for others and a low standard for ourselves. And Jesus calls that hypocrisy.

Imagine watching a video of your life. Assume every opinion you have, spoken or unspoken, becomes the standard you must meet. Have you been impatient with the person in the grocery line who tries to take thirteen items into the twelve-item line? As you watch your own video, will you pass your own grocery-store test? If you complain that your kids are ungrateful for all the financial support you provide, will running old footage of you reveal a young adult who consistently expressed gratitude for financial help? If you give a thumbs-down on the choices wealthy people make, how will you do when you watch the part about your own unexpected windfall?

If all your standards were applied to all your behavior, how would you fare?

If you're anything like me, you need to call the Doctor and schedule some major eye surgery.

MONDAY: OVERVIEW

1. Pray for insight, and then read Matthew 7:1–12.

> **Matthew 7:1** "Do not judge so that you will not be judged. **7:2** For by the standard you judge you will be judged, and the measure you use will be the measure you receive. **7:3** Why do you see the speck in your brother's eye, but fail to see the beam of wood in your own? **7:4** Or how can you say to your brother, 'Let me remove the speck from your eye,' while there is a beam in your own? **7:5** You hypocrite! First remove the beam from your own eye, and then you can see clearly to remove the speck from your brother's eye. **7:6** Do not give what is holy to dogs or throw your pearls before pigs; otherwise they will trample them under their feet and turn around and tear you to pieces.

7:7 "Ask and it will be given to you; seek and you will find; knock and the door will be opened for you. **7:8** For everyone who asks receives, and the one who seeks finds, and to the one who knocks, the door will be opened. **7:9** Is there anyone among you who, if his son asks for bread, will give him a stone? **7:10** Or if he asks for a fish, will give him a snake? **7:11** If you then, although you are evil, know how to give good gifts to your children, how much more will your Father in heaven give good gifts to those who ask him! **7:12** In everything, treat others as you would want them to treat you, for this fulfills the law and the prophets."

2. What questions come to mind as you read these verses?

_____

_____

_____

_____

_____

3. What topics does Jesus address in this week's reading?

_____

_____

_____

_____

_____

4. What part stands out as the section most needing your attention at this phase of your life?

_____

_____

_____

_____

_____

5. Who, if anyone, in your life can you ask whether others perceive you as being critical?

_____

_____

_____

_____

6. Spend some time praying for the Lord to reveal your double standards.

TUESDAY: THE JUDGE IN THE MIRROR

1. Pray that the Lord will help you to live by the same standards you expect of others. Then read today's verses several times:

> **Matthew 7:1** "Do not judge so that you will not be judged. **7:2** For by the standard you judge you will be judged, and the measure you use will be the measure you receive."

2. Jesus uses the word "for" suggesting a reason (Matt. 7:2). Why does He say His disciples should not judge?

_____

_____

_____

_____

3. What sort of judgment do you think He has in mind? Is He saying it's unchristian for a nation to have a public legal system? Why or why not?

_____

_____

_____

_____

4. What kinds of judgments were Christ-followers exhorted to make, according to the passages below?

> **1 Corinthians 5:1** It is actually reported that sexual immorality exists among you, the kind of immorality that is not permitted even among the Gentiles, so that someone is cohabiting with his father's wife. **5:2** And you are proud! Shouldn't you have been deeply sorrowful instead and removed the one who did this from among you? **5:3** For even though I am absent physically, I am present in spirit. And I have already judged the one who did this, just as though I were present. **5:4** When you gather together in the name of our Lord Jesus, and I am with you in spirit, along with the power of our Lord Jesus, **5:5** turn this man over to Satan for the destruction of the flesh, so that his spirit may be saved in the day of the Lord.

_____

_____

_____

_____

> **Galatians 5:6** For in Christ Jesus neither circumcision nor uncircumcision carries any weight—the only thing that matters is faith working through love. **5:7** You were running well; who prevented you from obeying the truth? **5:8** This persuasion does not come from the one who calls you! **5:9** A little yeast makes the whole batch of dough rise! **5:10** I am confident in the Lord that you

will accept no other view. But the one who is confusing you will pay the penalty, whoever he may be. **5:11** Now, brothers and sisters, if I am still preaching circumcision, why am I still being persecuted? In that case the offense of the cross has been removed. **5:12** I wish those agitators would go so far as to castrate themselves!

      John 7:21 Jesus replied, "I performed one miracle and you are all amazed. **7:22** However, because Moses gave you the practice of circumcision (not that it came from Moses, but from the forefathers), you circumcise a male child on the Sabbath. **7:23** But if a male child is circumcised on the Sabbath so that the law of Moses is not broken, why are you angry with me because I made a man completely well on the Sabbath? **7:24** Do not judge according to external appearance, but judge with proper judgment."

---

      1 John 4:1 Dear friends, do not believe every spirit, but test the spirits to determine if they are from God, because many false prophets have gone out into the world.

---

5. To find out what the word "judge" means as Jesus uses it in Matthew 7:1, it's helpful to know that it can have a range of meanings from making judicial decisions to having a judgmental attitude. But the context argues for "critical spirit" or "condemning attitude." "Judge" is used the same way in Romans 14:10–13.

> **Romans 14:10** But you who eat vegetables only—why do you judge your brother or sister? And you who eat everything—why do you despise your brother or sister? For we will all stand before the judgment seat of God. **14:11** For it is written, "*As I live, says the Lord, every knee will bow to me, and every tongue will give praise to God.*" **14:12** Therefore, each of us will give an account of himself to God. **14:13** Therefore we must not pass judgment on one another, but rather determine never to place an obstacle or a trap before a brother or sister.

A. What appears to be a parallel term for judgment, according to verse 10?

_____

B. How is judgment further clarified in verse 13?

_____

_____

_____

_____

6. Are you guilty of having a critical spirit? Do you look down on others, considering yourself better? List critical thoughts that have come to mind. Do you need to confront, confess, or let it go?

_____

_____

_____

_____

_____

_____

7. Is there someone who has been injured by your critical spirit and from whom you need to seek forgiveness?

_____

_____

_____

_____

WEDNESDAY: WOOD THEOLOGY

1. Read the following verses several times, and pray that the Lord will help you apply them:

> **Matthew 7:3** Why do you see the speck in your brother's eye, but fail to see the beam of wood in your own? **7:4** Or how can you say to your brother, 'Let me remove the speck from your eye,' while there is a beam in your own? **7:5** You hypocrite! First remove the beam from your own eye, and then you can see clearly to remove the speck from your brother's eye.

2. Consider the analogy Jesus uses. What's the difference in size between a speck (or "mote"–King James Version [KJV]) and a beam?

_____

_____

_____

3. What do you think is Jesus' point in setting up such a great contrast?

_____

_____

_____

_____

_____

4. Remember the last time you had to remove a splinter. How would having a beam in your eye prevent you from doing the job well?

_____

_____

_____

5. What does Jesus have to say about the continuity of the beam's presence (v. 4)?

_____

_____

_____

6. What name does Jesus give to the person who is critical of others' sins when he or she has an even bigger problem with the same sins (v. 5)?

_____

_____

7. We see an example of such hypocrisy in the life of King David. After he impregnates Bathsheba, Uriah's wife, he makes sure Uriah is killed in battle. So the prophet Nathan confronts David.

> So the Lord sent Nathan to David. When he came to him, Nathan said, "There were two men in a certain city, one rich and the

other poor. The rich man had a great many flocks and herds. But the poor man had nothing except for a little lamb he had acquired. He raised it, and it grew up alongside him and his children. It used to eat his food, drink from his cup, and sleep in his arms. It was just like a daughter to him.

"When a traveler came to the rich man, he did not want to use one of his own sheep or cattle to feed the traveler who had come to him. Instead, he took the poor man's lamb and fed it to the man who had come to him."

Then David became very angry at this man. He said to Nathan, "As surely the Lord lives, the man who did this deserves to die! Because he committed this cold-hearted crime, he must pay for the lamb four times over."

Nathan said to David, "You are that man! This is what the Lord God of Israel says: 'I chose you to be king over Israel and I rescued you from the hand of Saul.'" (2 Sam. 12:1–7)

Why do you think Nathan told David this story?

_____

_____

_____

_____

8. Consider Nathan's actions. According to Jesus, are His followers to allow the speck to remain in a brother's eye? What does He suggest as a plan of action (see Matt. 7:5)?

_____

_____

_____

_____

_____

9. Proverbs 27:6 says "Faithful are the wounds of a friend, but the kisses of an enemy are excessive." In Ephesians 4:15 we read that we're to speak the truth in love. What is the danger of speaking the truth without love? What is the danger in loving without speaking the truth?

_____

_____

_____

_____

_____

THURSDAY: THESE DOGS AND PIGS AREN'T PETS

1. Prayerfully read the verse for today several times:

> **Matthew 7:6** Do not give what is holy to dogs or throw your pearls before pigs; otherwise they will trample them under their feet and turn around and tear you to pieces.

2. Keep in mind that in the verses just prior to these, Jesus has just spoken of what needs to happen before going to a brother about his fault. In the context of confronting someone, why do you think Jesus would warn about the futility of trying to give to the unappreciative what is valuable?

_____

_____

_____

_____

3. Re-read Matthew 7:1–6.

A. How many verses in this section are spent discussing critical people?

_____

_____

B. How many are spent on those who are undiscriminating?

_____

_____

C. Why do you think Jesus spends more time focusing on one than the other?

_____

_____

_____

_____

_____

4. To what two animals does Jesus liken unreceptive people?

_____

_____

_____

_____

5. Today people have pet dogs and pet pigs. But keep in mind that dogs were not the household pets in Jesus' day that they are today. Dogs were considered more like wolves.

A. What do you know of how Jewish people felt and feel about pigs?

_____

_____

_____

_____

B. What does Jesus say these dogs and pigs are capable of doing?

_____

_____

C. How might knowing the way Jesus viewed these animals help your understanding of His meaning?

_____

_____

_____

6. We probably shouldn't understand Jesus' reference to "throwing" pearls as throwing pearls *at* the dogs and pigs as one throws rocks. Rather, we should probably understand Him as referring to those who try to feed or give jewels to these animals. To whom are pearls valuable? How do you think a dog or pig would respond to the taste and texture of pearls?

_____

_____

_____

_____

7. According to Jesus, what are the two dangers in throwing pearls to dogs and swine?

_____

_____

_____

_____

8. According to the passages that follow, what characterizes people who are a waste of time to try to reach?

Matthew 15:12–14

15:12 Then the disciples came to him and said, "Do you know that when the Pharisees heard this saying they were offended?" **15:13** And he replied, "Every plant that my heavenly Father did not plant will be uprooted. **15:14** Leave them! They are blind guides. If someone who is blind leads another who is blind, both will fall into a pit."

_____

_____

Acts 18:5–7

18:5 Now when Silas and Timothy arrived from Macedonia, Paul became wholly absorbed with proclaiming the word, testifying to the Jews that Jesus was the Christ. **18:6** When they opposed him and reviled him, he protested by shaking out his clothes and said to them, "Your blood be on your own heads! I am guiltless! From now on I will go to the Gentiles!" **18:7** Then Paul left the synagogue and went to the house of a person named Titius Justus, a Gentile who worshiped God, whose house was next door to the synagogue.

_____

_____

Titus 3:10 Reject a divisive person after one or two warnings.

_____

_____

9. Name some people in your life or in the culture at large who interact with Christians or Christian faith only to mock or express criticism. What are some Christlike ways to respond to such people?

_____

_____

_____

_____

_____

Friday: A Lesson from Parenting

By this time in Jesus' sermon those of His listeners with ears attentive to receive spiritual truth would be feeling overwhelmed by their need for God's grace, mercy, and forgiveness. Consider how uncomfortable it has been for us to face our own sin over the course of this five-week study. Imagine getting it all in one fifteen-minute dose. Recognizing that He would hold each of His listeners to the same standard by which they judge and by which they forgive, they would be focused on the bad-news part of the gospel: "I am a sinner!" It is in precisely this context that Jesus offers words of hope.

1. Ask the Lord to give you insight. Then read the verses we'll explore today.

> **Matthew 7:1** "Do not judge so that you will not be judged. **7:2** For by the standard you judge you will be judged, and the measure you use will be the measure you receive. **7:3** Why do you see the speck in your brother's eye, but fail to see the beam of wood in your own? **7:4** Or how can you say to your brother, 'Let me remove the

speck from your eye,' while there is a beam in your own? **7:5** You hypocrite! First remove the beam from your own eye, and then you can see clearly to remove the speck from your brother's eye. **7:6** Do not give what is holy to dogs or throw your pearls before pigs; otherwise they will trample them under their feet and turn around and tear you to pieces.

7:7 "Ask and it will be given to you; seek and you will find; knock and the door will be opened for you. **7:8** For everyone who asks receives, and the one who seeks finds, and to the one who knocks, the door will be opened. **7:9** Is there anyone among you who, if his son asks for bread, will give him a stone? **7:10** Or if he asks for a fish, will give him a snake? **7:11** If you then, although you are evil, know how to give good gifts to your children, how much more will your Father in heaven give good gifts to those who ask him! **7:12** In everything, treat others as you would want them to treat you, for this fulfills the law and the prophets.

2. Based on verse 11, it's clear that the asking, seeking, and knocking relate to asking something from your heavenly Father in prayer. What does the threefold approach to God (ask, seek, knock) assume about the level of passion on the part of those wanting something from Him?

_____

_____

_____

_____

_____

3. What three promises does Jesus give as recorded in Matthew 7:7–8? Why do you think He repeats himself?

_____

_____

_____

4. Notice that Jesus assumes that, having heard the Kingdom's requirements, His followers will ask God for help. What does this suggest about Jesus' confidence in their ability to achieve God's standard of perfection on their own?

_____

_____

_____

_____

5. Considering the context, what's wrong with claiming Matthew 7:7—"ask and you shall receive"—after praying for God to spare a loved one's life? Is He promise-bound to do so?

_____

_____

_____

_____

6. What two examples does Jesus give in which He likens a human parent to a child asking for food (see v. 10)? What should we assume is the answer to His rhetorical questions?

_____

_____

7. What parallel does Jesus make between earthly fathers and God as Heavenly Father (see v. 11)?

_____

_____

8. What word does Jesus use to describe those of His listeners who are earthly fathers (see v. 11)? Why do you think He says that of them?

_____

_____

_____

_____

9. Finally Jesus wraps it all up. What is His one-sentence summary of the Law and the Prophets (see v. 12)?

_____

_____

10. Jesus is not trying to start something new. He's saying that this is what's always been true. Have you ever heard it said that the God of the Old Testament is cruel and warlike, while the God of the New Testament is loving and kind? How does such thinking square with Jesus' words?

_____

_____

_____

11. Describe how you would love to be treated by others. How do you want people to handle your birthday and special events? To treat your confidential information? To act toward you at the office? Interact with you at home and at church? In a court of law? In your buying and selling transactions? In traffic? When you've wronged them? When you've messed up?

_____

_____

_____

_____

_____

_____

_____

12. How close does your description match up with how you treat others?

_____

_____

_____

_____

_____

_____

13. Spend some time asking, seeking, knocking. Ask God's forgiveness and mercy for yourself and others. Ask Him to transform you. Ask Him to make your life one that brings Him glory.

SATURDAY: THE PINK MINNIE MOUSE UMBRELLA

Scripture: "If you then, although you are evil, know how to give good gifts to your children, how much more will your Father in heaven give good gifts to those who ask him!" (Matt. 7:11)

One afternoon while I sat on the couch chatting with a friend, my four-year-old daughter sitting at a table nearby suddenly interrupted.

"Mommy, Mommy, look! I've got peas like a river!"

We turned and saw what she meant. There lined up in front of her was a row of carefully spaced little green frozen balls.

My friend and I exchanged knowing smiles. Then I started to say, "It's _peace_ like a river, honey—not peas." But I realized my daughter had it right after all. Considering how most of the rest of the world lives, we do have peas like a river. I can't remember a time when I ever had to skip a meal because we lacked food.

Our heavenly Father has more than met our needs. And since becoming a mom nearly ten years ago, I've seen a lot of parallels between human parenting and the spiritual parent-child relationship, especially when it comes to gift giving.

When my daughter's birthday rolls around, she won't find fourteen boxes of Girl Scout thin mints inside the gift wrap, even though she might beg for them. For Christmas when she is eleven, she won't discover software for unlimited Internet access under the tree. And I'm pretty sure that when she turns sixteen and can get her driver's license, we won't be surprising her with her own Kawasaki. It's not that I want to keep her from having fun. Quite the contrary. That's why my husband and I plot to give her good gifts—gifts that will delight her but that are also designed with her well being in view.

One such gift comes to mind. When she was five years old, she needed a new umbrella. Hers had broken along about Thanksgiving, and we had found it necessary to sneak its many pieces out of the house when she wasn't looking, because she couldn't bear to part with it. Soon after that, my husband found a pink Minnie Mouse umbrella with a big ruffle on sale. He knew she would love it the minute she saw, so he bought it and hid it in the back of our van until Christmas.

The first week of December we asked her, "What would you like for Christmas?"

She gave us a list of toys.

"Wouldn't you love a new umbrella?" we prompted.

"Oh, yes! I would love that! Are you giving me one?"

We shrugged. "It sure would be neat to have one, though, wouldn't it?"

The following week we asked, "If you got a new umbrella, what color would you want it to be?"

"I don't care."

"Well, I don't know about you, but I think pink would be the absolute best. Of course, most umbrellas we see are black. But it seems like pink would be much more fun."

"Oh, yes—pink would be wonderful!" she said. "Are you getting me one?"

We shrugged.

The week before Christmas we said, "If we were to get you a black umbrella, is there anything special you would want on it?"

"Well, I'd really rather have pink. But maybe a Barney the Dinosaur umbrella would be nice."

"Hmm—most umbrellas we see are black," we told her. "But wouldn't it be fun to have one with Minnie Mouse on it?"

"I *love* Minnie Mouse!" she exclaimed. "A pink Minnie Mouse umbrella would be the *best!*"

"Hey, as long as we're dreaming, wouldn't it be fun if it were pink *and* had Minnie Mouse *and* on top of that had a ruffle?"

"It would be the most beautiful umbrella in the world!" By now she was nearly swooning. Gift-giving is my daughter's love language.

Christmas Day finally arrived, and we saved the umbrella for last. The delight in her eyes and the glee in her voice when she opened it was every parent's dream. And that afternoon as we strolled down the street to go share dinner with our neighbors, our daughter toted her pink ruffled Minnie Mouse umbrella. Even though it was a beautiful day out, she had it up. She said she needed the shade from the sun. No way was she parting with her new treasure.

That night as we tucked her into bed and gave her a kiss, our arms felt something hard beneath the covers. Pulling them back, we found her umbrella safely tucked next to her as if it were a favorite doll.

Desire planted, desire fulfilled.

Jesus says we are evil parents—and we are. We get frustrated far too easily, we're less patient than we ought to be, and we sometimes make our children wait twenty minutes when we've told them, "Just a minute." But that doesn't stop us from giving good gifts.

If we, being evil, give good gifts, how much more will our heavenly Father give us good gifts? He will plant in us the desire to hunger and thirst after righteousness, to forgive others, to discern where best to invest pearls for His kingdom—gifts far more precious than whatever we might consider equivalent to the pink umbrella. And then He'll delight in answering our requests when we say we want these things. We have only to ask, seek, knock.

Prayer: *Heavenly Father, increase my desire for good things. Give me a heart to long for righteousness, to think critically without being critical, to examine myself that I might be in a position to offer help to others. Forgive me for falling short of my own standard, and help me to forgive others who have. Help me to hold myself to my own standards without* *hypocrisy while offering grace to those who don't fulfill my expectations. Grant me the desire to pursue hard after You—to keep on asking, keep on seeking, keep on knocking. In the name of Your gracious Son I pray. Amen.*

For Memorization: "In everything, treat others as you would want them to treat you, for this fulfills the law and the prophets." (Matt. 7:12)

WEEK 6 OF 6

A Study in Contrasts: Matthew 7:13–29

Scripture: "So in everything, do to others what you would have them do to you, for this sums up the Law and the Prophets." (Matt. 7:12)

"Most of us are umpires at heart," wrote Leo Aikman in the *Atlanta Constitution*. "We like to call balls and strikes on somebody else."[6]

It's easy to think the Golden Rule, doing to others as we would have them do to us, is a great way to live—until we have to live by it! Because we're so self-deceived, it's easier to spot where others foul up than to see our own flaws.

We say, "See? I knew that would happen"—yet we grit our teeth when people say to us, "I told you so."

We give our opinions whether or not people ask for them; then we get bent out of shape when others dispense unsolicited advice.

We get angry when our friends break confidences, yet we some-

[6] As cited at <www.yourquotations.net> and www.zaadz.net/quotes/authors/leo_aikman/ accessed January 11, 2006.

times reveal more than we should about them.

We feel jealous when others prosper, yet we expect them to rejoice when we have good news.

We call the people who speed by us "idiots" and the pokey people who go under the speed limit "morons," but then we exceed the speed limit when we're in a hurry and go under the speed limit when we get engrossed in conversation.

We criticize our spouses or bosses or in-laws for being unwilling to apologize, yet we have to choke out the words if we even admit when we're wrong.

We expect others to return favors, yet we hate it when they give to us with strings attached.

To avoid responsibility, we shift blame to others, yet we're outraged when people blame us for the consequences of their actions.

We get upset when people say, "I'm sorry, but . . ." or "I'm sorry if . . ." when we can't even seem to form the words "I'm sorry."

When we hear others cursing, we think they're unspiritual; yet we allow unkind, unedifying words to slip out of our mouths.

We assign motives to others, assuming they meant to hurt us, yet we demand that they give us the benefit of the doubt.

We notice and think "Tsk" when others pile their plates too high at buffet dinners, but we ourselves consume far more than the rest of the world.

We criticize our leaders, but we feel crushed when others point the finger at us without having all the facts.

We get our feelings hurt when others fail to see our pain, yet we turn a deaf ear to the pain experienced by most of the world.

We pick apart the pastor's sermon, but we couldn't preach a message to save our lives.

We expect others to read our minds, yet we get upset when they expect us to discern what they want.

In His Sermon on the Mount, Jesus let His followers know they were far too comfortable with their low double-standards. And we're just like them.

To truly live by the Golden Rule means living in a constant state of discomfort with ourselves. "I didn't go to religion to make me happy," wrote C. S. Lewis in *God in the Dock*. "I always knew a bottle of Port would do that. If you want a religion to make you feel comfortable, I certainly don't recommend Christianity."

Living as Christ demands also requires us to become some of the most imaginative people on earth. One of the ways my husband "de-escalates" conflict during moments of marital tension is to hear me out completely and then say, "I can see how you could see it that way." Often he may still disagree after he's listened. Yet when I know he has imagined himself in my high heels (so to speak), considered the situation from my perspective, and found my point of view reasonable, I feel treated with dignity even if in the end we decide against my recommended course of action.

Treating others as Christ would have us treat them means harnessing our imaginations so we can picture another's point of view. Imagine you are one of your friends, your spouse, one of your kids, or your boss. Put yourself in their slippers, golf shoes, soccer shoes, or expensive lace-ups. How would you see yourself? Are you an umpire or a team player?

MONDAY: OVERVIEW

1. Ask the Lord to give you insight into the text. Then read Matthew 7:13–28 twice.

> **7:13** "Enter through the narrow gate, because the gate is wide and the way is spacious that leads to destruction, and there are many who enter through it. **7:14** But the gate is narrow and the way is difficult that leads to life, and there are few who find it.
>
> **7:15** "Watch out for false prophets, who come to you in sheep's clothing but inwardly are voracious wolves. **7:16** You will recognize them by their fruit. Grapes are not gathered from thorns or figs from thistles, are they? **7:17** In the same way, every good tree bears good fruit, but the bad tree bears bad fruit. **7:18** A good tree is not able to bear bad fruit, nor a bad tree to bear good fruit. **7:19** Every tree that does not bear good fruit is cut down and thrown into the fire. **7:20** So then, you will recognize them by their fruit.
>
> **7:21** "Not everyone who says to me, 'Lord, Lord,' will enter into the kingdom of heaven—only the one who does the will of my Father in heaven. **7:22** On that day, many will say to me, 'Lord, Lord, didn't we prophesy in your name, and in your name cast out demons and do many powerful deeds?' **7:23** Then I will declare to them, 'I never knew you. Go away from me, you lawbreakers!'
>
> **7:24** "Everyone who hears these words of mine and does them is like a wise man who built his house on rock. **7:25** The rain fell, the flood came, and the winds beat against that house, but it did

not collapse because it had been founded on rock. **7:26** Everyone who hears these words of mine and does not do them is like a foolish man who built his house on sand. **7:27** The rain fell, the flood came, and the winds beat against that house, and it collapsed; it was utterly destroyed!"

7:28 When Jesus finished saying these things, the crowds were amazed by his teaching, **7:29** because he taught them like one who had authority, not like their experts in the law.

2. Jesus concludes His sermon with four sets of two contrasts.

A. What are the two gates (vv. 13–14)?

_____

_____

_____

_____

B. What are the two trees (vv. 17–20)?

_____

_____

_____

C. What are the two claims (vv. 21–23)?

_____

_____

_____

_____

D. What are the two foundations (vv. 24–27)?

_____

_____

_____

3. Put them all together, and what is Jesus' message?

_____

_____

_____

4. Do you think Jesus is teaching that His followers can be good enough to get into the kingdom of heaven based on diligent human effort? Or do you think He wants them to see how far they fall short of God's standard?

_____

_____

_____

_____

5. Based on all you've read in the Sermon on the Mount, why do you suppose God hates self-righteousness so much?

_____

_____

_____

_____

6. What do Matthew 7:21, 24, 26 suggest will characterize the person eligible to enter the Kingdom?

_____

_____

_____

_____

7. Which of the Lord's commands have you heard but not heeded? List them here. Then pray for His enabling to obey.

_____

_____

_____

TUESDAY: FRUIT OR FRUITCAKE?

1. Pray that the Spirit would illuminate His Word. Then read today's verses several times. Consider memorizing them:

> **Matthew 7:13** "Enter through the narrow gate, because the gate is wide and the way is spacious that leads to destruction, and there are many who enter through it. **7:14** But the gate is narrow and the way is difficult that leads to life, and there are few who find it.

2. How does Jesus describe the two gates? How does He describe the two roads?

_____

_____

_____

3. Where do the two gates and two roads lead? Note that "life" is a synonym for the kingdom of heaven.

_____

_____

_____

_____

4. Lose the "numbers" mentality.

A. Which of the two ways is the more populated course?

_____

_____

_____

B. Why do you think that is?

_____

_____

_____

_____

C. What is a weakness in the inclination to measure success in numbers?

_____

_____

_____

_____

5. Based on Jesus' words, are most people going to be in the kingdom of heaven, or only a minority?

_____

_____

6. Contrast what Jesus says in verses 13–14 with a "Majority rules" system. How do the two differ? What would you say most people think is the way to the kingdom of heaven?

_____

_____

_____

_____

7. If we follow Jesus, what should we expect from the majority?

_____

_____

_____

_____

8. List ways you're sometimes tempted to please people rather than God.

_____

_____

_____

_____

9. If you were to "enter by the gate and walk the narrow way," how might your life look different?

_____

_____

_____

_____

_____

WEDNESDAY: THE "RED RIDING HOOD" WARNING

1. Pray for insight. Then read today's verses several times:

> **Matthew 7:15** "Watch out for false prophets, who come to you in sheep's clothing but inwardly are voracious wolves **7:16** You will recognize them by their fruit. Grapes are not gathered from thorns or figs from thistles, are they? **7:17** In the same way, every good tree bears good fruit, but the bad tree bears bad fruit. **7:18** A good tree is not able to bear bad fruit, nor a bad tree to bear good fruit. **7:19** Every tree that does not bear good fruit is cut down and thrown into the fire. **7:20** So then, you will recognize them by their fruit.

2. According to verse 15, what are false prophets like on the outside? On the inside? What word does Jesus use to describe the wolves?

_____

_____

_____

_____

_____

3. What is the danger when a false teacher seems harmless on the outside?

_____

_____

_____

_____

4. What are some ways false teachers dupe people? Name some false teachings common today (for example, "Follow Jesus and you'll get rich").

_____

_____

_____

_____

5. Based on the context of Sermon on the Mount, one characteristic that might qualify someone as a false teacher would be advocating a "wide way" and "confidence of spirit" as Kingdom requirements.

A. Have you encountered the teaching that contends that there are many ways to God? Have you thought this yourself?

_____

_____

_____

_____

_____

B. Have you ever encountered the idea that we shouldn't make people feel uncomfortable about their sin? Have you yourself believed this?

_____

_____

_____

6. If someone has it together externally, it's difficult to discern if his or her teaching is sound. What phrase does Jesus repeat when telling His followers how they can know who's sound and who's not (vv. 16, 20)?

_____

_____

_____

7. Jesus speaks metaphorically of fruit.

A. What do you think He means on a literal level? That is, how will His followers be able to determine who has sound teaching?

_____

_____

_____

_____

B. Do you think by "fruit" He means external success and large followings?

_____

_____

_____

8. Whenever you see "in the same way" in Scripture (v. 17), ask, "In the same way as what?" What was Jesus saying in the verse that directly precedes verse 17?

_____

_____

_____

_____

9. What happens to the tree that doesn't bear good fruit (see v. 19)?

_____

_____

10. What about your own beliefs, ideas, and/or teachings? Have they been in line with what Jesus says? How so or how not?

_____

_____

_____

_____

_____

_____

_____

_____

11. Think of the story of Red Riding Hood and how it illustrates the idea of a wolf dressed in disguise. If you enjoy using your sanctified imagination, write out your own short parable or fairy tale to illustrate one of the truths in this section.

_____

_____

_____

_____

_____

_____

THURSDAY: THE WILL TO LIVE

1. Pray that the Lord would speak to you through His Word. Then slowly read the following verses three times, meditating on the truth in them.

> **Matthew 7:21** "Not everyone who says to me, 'Lord, Lord,' will enter into the kingdom of heaven—only the one who does the will of my Father in heaven. **7:22** On that day, many will say to me, 'Lord, Lord, didn't we prophesy in your name, and in your name cast out demons and do many powerful deeds?' **7:23** Then I will declare to them, 'I never knew you. Go away from me, you lawbreakers!' "

2. Self-delusion and measuring by externals are two dangers for those who profess faith.

A. Rather than seeing your ongoing spiritual bankruptcy, have you placed confidence in your good works as measures of your spirituality and that of others? If so, how?

_____

_____

_____

_____

B. Have you measured the success of your and others' spirituality by externals rather than by the standards set forth in the Beatitudes? If so, how?

_____

_____

_____

_____

C. Do you value others' spirituality based on their accomplishments, such as having attended seminary, written books, or spoken at conferences? What does God value?

_____

_____

_____

_____

3. Notice the personal pronouns Jesus uses in verse 21.

A. What does this say about Jesus' involvement in determining who will and won't enter the kingdom?

_____

_____

_____

_____

B. What does His involvement at the judgment say about His divinity?

_____

_____

_____

4. What does Jesus say is the kingdom entrance requirement (v. 21)?

_____

_____

_____

5. Will many or few find they've deceived themselves (v. 22)? Does this disturb you?

_____

_____

_____

_____

6. What three types of "externals" does Jesus say will have been performed by the deceived (v. 22)?

_____

_____

_____

_____

7. What two things will Jesus say to those who have not done God's will (v. 23)?

_____

_____

_____

8. Jesus' words are remarkably similar to those of the psalmist at the end of Psalm 6.

A. Read the psalm:

> **Psalm 6:1** Lord, do not rebuke me in your anger! Do not punish me in your raging fury!
>
> **6:2** Have mercy on me, Lord, for I am frail! Heal me, Lord, for my bones are shaking!
>
> **6:3** I am absolutely terrified, and you, Lord—how long will this go on?
>
> **6:4** Come back, Lord, rescue me! Deliver me because of your faithfulness!
>
> **6:5** For no one mentions your name in the realm of death, In Sheol who gives you thanks?
>
> **6:6** I am exhausted as I groan; all night long I drench my bed in tears; my tears saturate the cushion beneath me.
>
> **6:7** My eyes grow dim from suffering; they grow weak because of all my enemies.
>
> **6:8** Turn back from me, all you who behave wickedly, for the Lord has heard the sound of my weeping!
>
> **6:9** The Lord has heard my appeal for mercy; the Lord has accepted my prayer.
>
> **6:10** May all my enemies be humiliated and absolutely terrified! May they turn back and be suddenly humiliated!

It's difficult to tell whether the psalmist is near death because of illness or because he's under the discipline of the Lord. Either way, his enemies have mocked him in his humbled state. Note that he has wept and cried for mercy. Then somehow he has received a word from the Lord—whether by means of a prophet, a dream, or one of the various ways God spoke in Old Testament times (see Heb. 1:1)—and has assurance that his prayer is accepted.

B. Why did he say his eyes were failing (Psalm 6:7)?

_____

_____

_____

C. What's similar about what the psalmist says in verse 8 and Jesus' words in Matthew 7:23?

_____

_____

_____

_____

D. What three things does the psalmist say will happen to his enemies? (v. 10)

_____

_____

_____

Jesus is probably referring to this psalm in His sermon. If so, by making the link, He connects those who come to Him saying, "Lord, Lord" but have not done God's will with those who have mocked humility. They are self-deceived and numbered among the enemies of His people.

9. Many say Christianity is a crutch for those who need help. After studying the Sermon on the Mount, would you agree? Why or why not?

_____

_____

_____

1. Pray for wisdom from God to understand the text. Then read these verses:

> **Matthew 7:24** "Everyone who hears these words of mine and does them is like a wise man who built his house on rock. **7:25** The rain fell, the flood came, and the winds beat against that house, but it did not collapse because it had been founded on rock. **7:26** Everyone who hears these words of mine and does not do them is like a foolish man who built his house on sand. **7:27** The rain fell, the flood came, and the winds beat against that house, and it collapsed; it was utterly destroyed!"
>
> **7:28** When Jesus finished saying these things, the crowds were amazed by his teaching, **7:29** because he taught them like one who had authority, not like their experts in the law.

2. Compare Matthew 7:21 (in yesterday's study) with 7:24. How are they similar?

_____

_____

_____

_____

_____

3. On what are the two houses built (vv. 24, 26)?

_____

4. What does the first house endure (v. 25)?

_____

_____

5. What does the second house endure (v. 27)?

_____

_____

6. In the end, what happens to each house?

_____

_____

_____

_____

7. Do both sets of people hear Jesus' words? What's different about them (vv. 24–27)?

_____

_____

_____

_____

_____

8. Do you meet the kingdom entry requirements? That is, do you hear Jesus' words and obey? Does your righteousness exceed that of the scribes and the Pharisees? Are you perfect as your heavenly Father is perfect? Do you do the will of the Father? Do you hunger and thirst for righteousness? Are you meek? If you fall short, ask for the grace of

Christ to make up the difference between God's standard and your holiness.

_____

_____

_____

_____

9. Why were the people amazed when Jesus finished (vv. 28–29)?

_____

_____

_____

_____

_____

10. What gave Jesus the right to speak with authority and to contradict the religious leaders when He was not even a trained expert in the law?

_____

_____

_____

_____

_____

SATURDAY: JESUS AND PAUL

Scripture: "So then, be perfect, as your heavenly Father is perfect." (Matt. 5:48)

A few months back I saw an old friend at a funeral. She had left her husband and kids to move in with her lesbian lover—something I had a lot of difficulty understanding, especially because this friend and I once went together on a mission trip to Mexico.

"So what do you believe about the Bible now?" I asked. "What do you do with Romans 1?"

"Ah," she smiled. "I believe only in Jesus' words—not Paul's. And Jesus never condemned homosexuality."

The perceived gap between Jesus and Paul widens when we talk about how people are saved. It's said that Paul taught salvation by grace through faith in Christ alone and that Jesus taught something different. After all, the Beatitudes don't exactly sound like "Believe in Me, and you'll be saved."

Yet if we understand Jesus as ultimately teaching anything but salvation by grace through faith alone, the kingdom of God will have a King but zero subjects. Who would make it in? Remember His requirements—"Be perfect as your heavenly Father is perfect" and "unless your righteousness exceeds that of the scribes and the Pharisees" and "only those who do the will of my Father . . ." And lest we think we've reached the perfect standard, we get hit with "Blessed are the meek," which reveals our pride. Put all these together and you have the entire world standing condemned—which is precisely what Paul says in Romans 3:

> **3:10** Just as it is written:
> "There is no one righteous, not even one,
> **3:11** there is no one who understands,
> there is no one who seeks God.
> **3:12** All have turned away,
> together they have become worthless;
> there is no one who shows kindness, not even one."

And lest we think he's making up something new, he continues to quote the Old Testament:

> **3:13** "Their throats are open graves,
> they deceive with their tongues,
> The poison of asps is under their lips."
> **3:14** "Their mouths are full of cursing and bitterness."
> **3:15** "Their feet are swift to shed blood,
> **3:16** ruin and misery are in their paths,
> **3:17** and the way of peace they have not known."

3:18 "There is no fear of God before their eyes."

It's bad news all the way. He goes on:

3:19 Now we know that whatever the law says, it says to those who are under the law, so that every mouth may be silenced and the whole world may be held accountable to God. **3:20** For *no one is declared righteous before him* by the works of the law, for through the law comes the knowledge of sin.

Jesus' preaching let His listeners know they stood condemned. The Law was unchanged, but that left them all in trouble. And who of us, if we're honest, comes anywhere close to Jesus' standards? Through both Jesus' words to His followers and Paul's words to the church at Rome, we learn that the first step in understanding the good news is clearly to see the bad news: all have sinned.

Paul continues:

Romans 3:21 But now apart from the law the righteousness of God (which is attested by the law and the prophets) has been disclosed—**3:22** namely, the righteousness of God through the faithfulness of Jesus Christ for all who believe. For there is no distinction, **3:23** for all have sinned and fall short of the glory of God. **3:24** But they are justified freely by his grace through the redemption that is in Christ Jesus. **3:25** God publicly displayed him at his death as the mercy seat accessible through faith. This was to demonstrate his righteousness, because God in his forbearance had passed over the sins previously committed. **3:26** This was also to demonstrate his righteousness in the present time, so that he would be just and the justifier of the one who lives because of Jesus' faithfulness.

3:27 Where, then, is boasting? It is excluded! By what principle? Of works? No, but by the principle of faith!

The bad news is that we're sinners. We have an amazing propensity toward self-deception and self-righteousness, but when it comes to true righteousness, we're hopeless and helpless. Yet the good news is that the King himself bore the penalty for the crimes of His subjects. We're dead to the law through identification with His death in the same way that a wife is no longer bound to her husband once he has died. And we're raised in newness of life through identification with Jesus' resurrection. That new life is one of obedience to God's will, but not so we can add anything to what He has done. How could we possibly add to His righteousness, which is credited to every believer's account? Rather, we love because He first loved us.

Have you trusted Jesus Christ's payment for your sin and had His righteousness credited to your account? If you already know Him, are you maturing in the same way you were saved—by grace through faith?

Prayer: *Lord Jesus, how marvelously You demonstrated Your mercy to me when I was helpless. Forgive my pride! What possible reason could I have for boasting, except in the greatness of You who have done all for me? Amazing love! How can it be that You, my God, should die for me? Since You have bought me out of the slave market of sin and purchased me for yourself, You have every right to receive my obedience and worship and unswerving devotion. You alone—not my own filthy works—are my foundation. Please give me the strength to do the will of Your Father, to whom be the kingdom and the power and the glory forever. Amen.*

For Memorization: "Everyone who hears these words of mine and does them is like a wise man who built his house on rock. The rain fell, the flood came, and the winds beat against that house, but it did not collapse because it had been founded on rock." (Matt. 7:24–25)

About the NET BIBLE®

The NET BIBLE® is an exciting new translation of the Bible with 60,932 translators' notes! These translators' notes make the original Greek, Hebrew and Aramaic texts of the Bible far more accessible and unlocks the riches of the Bible's truth from entirely new perspectives.

The NET BIBLE® is the first modern Bible to be completely free for anyone, anywhere in the world to download as part of a powerful new "Ministry First" approach being pioneered at bible.org.

Download the entire NET Bible and
60,932 notes for free at www.bible.org

About the bible.org ministry

Before there was eBay® . . . before there was Amazon.com® . . . there was bible.org! Bible.org is a non-profit (501c3) Christian ministry headquartered in Dallas, Texas. In the last decade bible.org has grown to serve millions of individuals around the world and provides thousands of trustworthy resources for Bible study (2 Tim 2:2).

Go to www.bible.org for thousands
of trustworthy resources including:

- The NET BIBLE®
- Discipleship Materials
- The Theology Program
- More than 10,000 Sermon Illustrations
- ABC's of Christian Growth
- Bible Dictionaries and Commentaries